FINISHING
WELL

FINISHING
WELL

ELMER L. TOWNS

DESTINY IMAGE® PUBLISHERS, INC.
P.O. Box 310, Shippensburg, PA 17257-0310
"Promoting Inspired Lives."

This book and all other Destiny Image and Destiny Image Fiction books are available at Christian bookstores and distributors worldwide.

For more information on foreign distributors, call 717-532-3040.
Reach us on the Internet: www.destinyimage.com.

ISBN 13 TP: 978-0-7684-7468-8
ISBN 13 eBook: 978-0-7684-7489-3

For Worldwide Distribution.
1 2 3 4 5 6 7 8 / 28 27 26 25 24

CONTENTS

WHEN YOU HAVE FINISHED WELL

When the vision that motivated you to launch out on the project God has put upon your heart is complete and you have done what the vision expected, then you have *finished well*.

When the burden that motivated you to work, sacrifice, and endure suffering is lifted because you have completed what you have begun, then you have *finished well*.

When your life's challenge has been accomplished, and you moved into action to satisfy the demands of your challenge, then you have *finished well*.

When you have completed all that is required by your task, and you are satisfied that you have done your best, and you have completed the job, then you have *finished well*.

When you have done all that those over you have asked and/or expected, and you know they are satisfied with your work, then you have *finished well*.

When you know what the public expects of you and you have completed the task they expected you to finish, and you fulfilled their expectations, then you have *finished well*.

Introduction

To Cross the Finish Line

"Finish well," some will tell you. What do they mean when they admonish you to finish well?

If it is a long, hot, 26-mile marathon, and you have run halfway to the finish line, then finishing well means running to the end of the race—breaking the tape!

If you are trying to make the school track team and you are just an average runner, then you are challenged to do your best, improve, make the team, finish your dream well.

If you are working on a term paper and someone challenges you to finish well, what do they mean? It could mean getting an "A" from your professor. But that "A" might not be your best effort. Perhaps you only give half-effort to get an "A." Finishing well does not mean you write the best paper compared to anyone in the world. For you to finish well means to do your best, all the time, every time!

When God tells you to "finish well," what does He mean? First of all, you accepted Jesus Christ as your Savior, and you have begun walking in faith and obeying the Master. To "finish well" means you continue to walk with Him the rest of your life and complete what God has planned for your life. Remember the Lord said, *"I have a plan for your life, it is for your good and not to harm you"* (Jeremiah 29:11, ELT).

To finish well does not mean to be the best of everyone in the world. Finishing well is completing what you have started. Finishing well means completing your task on earth to the best of your knowledge and ability, and you finish on time.

Another person may think that finishing well is being at the head of the class. Another thinks it is being the best student in the whole school. Another may think finishing well means being the very best in the whole world. What is God asking when He expects you to finish well? He wants you to live the best (obedient) life you can, using all of the spiritual gifts you have, learning as much about Christ as possible, serving Him as best you can with your ability, being as faithful in attendance in church, ministry, and giving offerings to God. Finishing well does not mean sinless perfection. No! Not at all. It means following Christ, walking by faith, keeping your eyes on Him, and living in expectation of His any-moment return.

You have finished well when you have done everything God has asked, and you cannot do anything more. Now, cross the finish line!

CHAPTER 1

GRANDPA JACOB BLESSED HIS GRANDCHILDREN

Then Israel [Jacob] stretched out his right hand and laid it on Ephraim's head, who was the younger, and his left hand on Manasseh's head, guiding his hands knowingly, for Manasseh was the firstborn. "…Bless the lads; let my name be named upon them, and the name of my fathers Abraham and Isaac; and let them grow into a multitude in the midst of the earth."

Now when Joseph saw that his father laid his right hand on the head of Ephraim, it displeased him; so he took hold of his father's hand to remove it from Ephraim's head to Manasseh's head. And Joseph said to his father, "Not so, my father, for this one is the firstborn; put your right hand on his head."

But his father refused and said, "…his younger brother shall be greater than he, and his descendants shall become a multitude of nations"
(Genesis 48:14, 16–19).

Jacob did not begin well. As a matter of fact, he made many mistakes. When his older brother Esau came back from hunting and was hungry, Esau asked his younger brother Jacob for some of the red stew that was cooking on the fire. We know little about the stew except the smell must have enticed the older brother. Older brother Esau was starving so he asked for something to eat. This first glimpse into the life of Jacob gave him the name "deceiver."

Jacob could have been a good little brother by sharing his stew with his hungry brother, but he did not. He bargained for a future place of prominence with his brother: "*Sell me your birthright as of this day*" (Genesis 25:31). Both Esau and Jacob were young, and the birthright meant nothing to the older brother Esau. What he wanted at the time was to satisfy his hunger. The birthright meant leadership of the family, the decision-maker of important times, and to carry on the family traditions. So Esau gave his future to Jacob; now the second born owned the birthright.

Later, the father Isaac asked his older son Esau to go kill a deer, then cook the meat and bring it to him for a ceremonial meal. After the meal, the father would lay hands on the head of his oldest son, Esau, to give him the family inheritance. That meant ownership of all the cattle, tents—all the possessions.

The mother, Rebekah, overheard what her husband Isaac said to Esau. The problem is, "*Isaac loved Esau...but Rebekah loved Jacob*" (Genesis 25:28).

Quickly the mother devised a plan and drew her son Jacob into the plot. She had a young lamb killed and roasted. When young Jacob protested, his father would recognize the difference in taste, so she covered the meat with spices.

Again young Jacob objected, "*Esau my brother is a hairy man, and I am a smooth-skinned man*" (Genesis 27:11). Young Jacob went on to explain that his father would touch him, lay hands on him, and he would recognize the deception.

Rebekah solved that problem; she turned animal skins into a jacket with sleeves so that when the elderly Isaac—now blinded—touched his son Jacob, he would think it was Esau.

Even with the deception, Isaac seemed to know he was being deceived, saying, "*The voice is Jacob's voice, but the hands are the hands of Esau*" (Genesis 27:22).

The deception went well and Jacob was promised the family inheritance. When Esau found out, he wept and said, "*He has cheated me twice. First he took my rights as the firstborn, and now he has stolen my blessing*" (Genesis 27:36, ELT).

Then Esau determined to kill Jacob, but he planned to wait until Isaac died. The mother heard about Esau's plan and sent Jacob off to live with her brother—out of the Promised Land, across the Euphrates River, to the family where she was born and raised.

The deceiver Jacob went to work for his uncle Laban, brother to his mother. On several occasions, Jacob deceived his uncle Laban. While Jacob was the herdsman taking care of his uncle's flocks, he struck a deal that certain livestock that were born streaked, speckled, and gray-spotted would be his, but all the natural-born sheep belonged to his uncle. Jacob devised a plan by intermingling female sheep with streaked, speckled, and gray-spotted males. As a result the flock gave birth to a number of sheep that belonged to Jacob.

After twenty years of deceptions, Jacob planned to steal away from his uncle to return to the land of his birth across the Euphrates. Jacob planned to go back to the Promised Land and his people. He gathered all the animals and wealth he had acquired and silently left uncle Laban to go home.

Then young Jacob met older brother Esau coming to meet him. Jacob again tried to deceive Esau. He sent a certain number of his animals ahead as a gift to Esau. He sent them in different groups to placate the angry brother.

When Jacob and Esau met, Jacob's past sins were not an issue; their common birth and brotherhood brought them tighter. They did not fight and Esau did not attack Jacob. They departed with what now has been known as the Mizpah Benediction used by churches for centuries, *"May the Lord watch between you and me when we are absent one from another"* (Genesis 31:49).

While living beyond the Euphrates River with uncle Laban, Jacob had twelve sons and one daughter. He lived his life on the edge of desperation, but God still blessed him in spite of his dereliction.

In today's story, ancient Jacob is in Egypt. He is over 100 years old and is preparing to die. His son, Joseph, brings two grandsons to receive the blessing from Grandpa Jacob. He was very old, and Jacob propped himself up using his shepherd's staff for support so he could bless his two grandsons. He said, *"God Almighty appeared to me at Luz in the land of Canaan and blessed me"* (Genesis 48:3).

Jacob gave his testimony to his grandsons. And what is a testimony? It is a verbal statement that includes who you were before you met God and what you did to receive God's blessing in your life. But best/most of all it includes a request for God's blessing in the future. Today, your testimony is your life before conversion, what you did to receive Jesus Christ as Savior, and how God changed your life.

Notice Jacob reminded them of God's name, "God Almighty." Then he told them about the Abrahamic promise transferred to him. *"Behold, I the Lord will prosper you in all that you do. I will give you many children and you will become a great nation. I the Lord promise this land to you—a Promised Land—that you shall inherit this land for an everlasting possession"* (Genesis 48:4, ELT).

It was then that Grandpa Jacob told his grandsons about Grandma Rachel. They would not have known her, but he wanted them to know, *"when I came from Padan, Rachel died beside me in the land of Canaan on the way...I buried her there"* (Genesis 48:7).

FOUR THINGS GRANDPA JACOB DID FOR HIS GRANDCHILDREN

1. GRANDPA JACOB ADOPTED THEM.

Now the two sons of Joseph—Ephraim and Manasseh—were born to Joseph and his Egyptian wife. We are not sure how Jacob approved the marriage of Joseph, but he used the language of adoption to make sure everyone knew the two boys belonged to him and his heritage. *"And now your two sons, Ephraim and Manasseh...shall be mine"* (Genesis 48:5). Since this was recognized as an act of adoption, Ephraim and Manasseh became two of the twelve tribes of Israel. They took their place among the twelve tribes, and Jacob's heritage was guaranteed.

2. GRANDPA JACOB KISSED AND HUGGED THEM.

Jacob wanted them to know he loved them, cared for them, and that is why "*he kissed them and embraced them*" (Genesis 48:10). Perhaps this is the greatest expression of love from a grandfather to his grandchildren.

3. GRANDPA JACOB LAID HIS HAND ON THEM.

Jacob did a strange thing. Remember Jacob was the "deceiver," and here Grandpa Jacob was going to force his will on the adoption process and bestow the right of inheritance to the second son of Joseph. "*Then Israel* [Jacob] *stretched out his right hand and laid it on Ephraim's head, who was the younger, and his left hand on Manasseh's head...the firstborn*" (Genesis 48:14). Technically, the right hand should have gone on Manasseh's head because he was the older son and Ephraim the younger. But perhaps Jacob was looking at God's practice in his life. Jacob was the second born who was preferred before Esau, the firstborn. Remember, Jacob now had the leadership of God's people, not his older brother Esau.

4. GRANDPA JACOB BLESSED HIS GRANDCHILDREN.

Since the word *blessing* means to *add value* to the life of the one whom you are blessing, look at the result: "*By faith Jacob, when he was dying, blessed each of the sons of Joseph*" (Hebrews 11:21).

The Levitical Blessing
"The Lord bless you and keep you;
The Lord make His face shine upon you,
And be gracious to you;
The Lord lift up His countenance upon you,
And give you peace."
Numbers 6:24–26

How to Bless Children

1. **A meaningful touch.** It is important that you reach out and place your hands on the child you are blessing, whether they are your children, grandchildren, or great-grandchildren.

2. **Blessing with spoken words.** Let the children hear and understand what you are saying so they can apply it to their heart. You want them to remember and live according to what you have predicated.

3. **Attach high value to the one being blessed.** Too often parents create a negative self-image in their children when they tell them, "You are dumb" or "you never obey me" or another put-down. Don't do that. When you continually tear them down, where are they? Down! Do the opposite. By blessing them you lift them up with your expectations for them. You are telling them what you expect them to do in their lives and how they will achieve and have victory.

4. **Picture a special feature for the child being blessed.** Make sure the child understands that God loves them, has a plan for their life, and will guide them and use them (Jeremiah 31:11).

5. **An active commitment to fulfill the blessing.** More than words, the parent must put aside money to fund a child's education or other resources to get started in marriage or business. Other commitments include possessions such as property, a car, or other special family treasures.

Four Things Grandpa Jacob Gave Them

1. Grandpa Jacob gave them his name.

"Let my name be named upon them, and the name of my fathers Abraham and Isaac" (Genesis 48:16). In this act Jacob accepted both boys without hesitation, recognizing they had his blood flowing in their veins. Their life would fulfill his life. But more than fulfilling his life, what God promised Jacob, these children would carry out God's promise and pass it on to their children (Jacob's great-grandchildren).

When you give your grandchildren your name, you recognize they are not second-class family members. They are important to you, to history, and to the Lord's work.

You must love each one of them equally, so you make sure they realize they have your name, and they are proud of you and you of them.

2. GRANDPA JACOB GAVE GOD'S FUTURE TO THEM.

Because God has a plan for everyone, God had a plan for Ephraim and Manasseh. *"Let them grow into a multitude in the midst of the earth"* (Genesis 48:16).

3. GRANDPA JACOB GAVE THEM HIS LOVE.

And what is love? Love is giving yourself to the one you love. Jacob gave himself to his grandchildren without reserve. So, when you love your grandchildren, you open up your heart to them and you open your mind to them and you open up your treasures to them.

4. GRANDPA JACOB GAVE THEM AN EXAMPLE OF WORSHIP.

Technically he gave them two ways to worship. First, *"he bowed down with his face to the earth"* (Genesis 48:12). What went through these grandchildren's minds when they saw their grandfather on his face before God worshiping Him? That is a role model that is indelible.

Second, Jacob was *"leaning upon the top of his staff"* (Hebrews 11:21). He probably leaned on his staff for support as he blessed his grandchildren.

BLESSINGS TO TAKE AWAY

1. **Be concerned about your children's spiritual condition**. Also be concerned about how you can include them in your earthly possessions and money.

2. **Be a spiritual example** with your attitude, words, and actions.

3. **Give your testimony** to everyone including your grandchildren. Make sure each grandchild knows how you live for God and how they can serve God. Then challenge them to do it.

HOW TO BLESS YOUR CHILDREN AND GRANDCHILDREN BOTH NATURALLY AND SUPERNATURALLY

1. **Intention.** If you want to bless your children and grandchildren, it takes the dedication of your mind, emotions, and will. You must want to do it and you must want its results.

2. **Plan** to determine a time, place, and event when you can transfer your blessing to them.

3. **Make an appointment** for the time and place. When it is settled, tell them you are coming to bless them. Arrange to have other relatives present.

4. **Be intentional** about your blessing because God is watching. He knows what you are doing, as well as your children and grandchildren. Let them know how important God is to you and to them.

No matter who you are...how you began...what you have done... where you are now...you can finish well.

CHAPTER 2

GRANDMA NAOMI INFLUENCED GENERATIONS

The man's name was Elimelech, and his wife was Naomi. Their two sons were Mahlon and Chilion. They were Ephrathites from Bethlehem in the land of Judah. They left and went to the land of Moab; they settled there. Then Elimelech died, and Naomi was left with her two sons

(Ruth 1:2-3, ELT).

A COMPROMISING MOTHER BECOMES AN INFLUENCING GRANDMOTHER

Naomi and Elimelech were called Ephrathites, meaning blue bloods or upper class or, in our day, they were listed with the rich and the famous. In modern-day terminology they were well known, well respected, well-endowed.

Naomi and Elimelech were from Bethlehem, which means *house of bread*, but after they were married, Bethlehem was anything but a house of bread. *"There was a famine in the land"* (Ruth 1:1).

Naomi and Elimelech *"went to dwell in the country of Moab"* (Ruth 1:1). From their home in Bethlehem they could see the well-watered plains of Moab across the Jordan River. There was no famine in Moab, so they went to stay there a short period of time. Probably they were planning to make it through the famine then return home.

Elimelech went to Moab to keep from dying, but it was there he died. Some people will not give up anything (including money, homes, possessions) so they keep everything. But in the end they lose what they cannot keep, because they would not give (dedicate) it to the Lord in the first place. "*They* [Naomi and Elimelech] *went to the country of Moab and remained there*" (Ruth 1:2).

WHAT DID NAOMI LEAVE?

- She left the land of promise for a land of compromise.
- She left the temple in Jerusalem for a land of idols.
- She left the fellowship of God's people for unsaved heathen.
- She ran away from her problems, seeking an easy life, but the problems were in her heart. They followed her until she made a commitment to God.

Naomi and Elimelech had two sons who both married heathen women. If they were good Jewish believers, they would have understood that God's people were not to marry outside of their faith, i.e., not marry the heathen. Does that mean that Naomi and Elimelech did not teach their sons properly or influence them to live separated lives? Did Naomi and Elimelech encourage Mahlon to marry heathen Orpah and Chilion to marry Ruth?

After Naomi's husband died, she remained in Moab for a time with no purpose, no plans, no hope. Maybe she was waiting for grandchildren that her two sons would give her, but the children did not come. Also, both Mahlon and Chilion died, leaving Naomi with two daughters-in-laws.

THE DECISION

Naomi decided to return to the Promised Land, going back to her heritage and people. However, this was not a spiritual commitment to God. When Orpah and Ruth wanted to go with her, Naomi encouraged them to go back to their people, to their culture, and to their gods. Naomi gave wrong counsel for a Hebrew mother.

Orpah kissed her mother-in-law good-bye. But Ruth clung tightly to Naomi. "Look," Naomi said to her, "your sister-in-law has gone back to her people and to her gods. You should do the same." But Ruth replied, "Don't ask me to leave you and turn back. Wherever you go, I will go; wherever you live, I will live. Your people will be my people, and your God will be my God. Wherever you die, I will die, and there I will be buried. May the Lord punish me severely if I allow anything but death to separate us!"

(Ruth 1:14-17, NLT)

NAOMI'S COMPRISE

- Wrong place: went to Moab
- Wrong priority: money
- Wrong environment: tolerated Moab culture
- Wrong counsel: sent Orpah back to her old life and gods

Naomi came back to God's people with a critical spirit; God had yet to work in her heart the true transformation that she needed. She testified, *"I went out full, and the Lord has brought me home again empty"* (Ruth 1:21). The word *empty* meant that her husband was dead, her sons were both dead, one daughter-in-law left her, and all she had was Ruth.

NAOMI'S REPENTANCE SEEN IN HER ACTIONS

Naomi recognized God's punishment. Sometimes the first step of repentance is to recognize what you have done wrong. Then you must realize God was punishing you for being wrong. Naomi said, *"The Lord has caused me to suffer and the Almighty has sent such tragedy"* (Ruth 1:21, NLT).

After Naomi and Ruth arrived in Bethlehem, we read the story of Ruth going out looking for a place to work. God was working behind the details because He had a plan for both Ruth and Naomi. The Bible says that *"She [Ruth] happened to come to the part of the field belonging to*

Boaz, who was of the family of Elimelech" (Ruth 2:3). For Ruth to gather grain left by the harvesters was similar to begging for bread. Apparently Ruth did not know that she was gathering grain from the field of a distant relative of Elimelech. She basically was looking for any place she could find work, looking for food.

Boaz, a godly man, greeted his workers. "*The Lord be with you!*" and they answered, "*The Lord bless you!*" (Ruth 2:4). The Bible includes this apparently innocent greeting between workers and Boaz to show Boaz's spiritual outlook on life. Boaz was not in the line of the priesthood, nor was he a prophet or in the line of leadership. He was simply a man whom God had blessed, and so Boaz turned to bless God.

The law of kinsmen redeemer was on the books describing a levirate marriage, which required a man to marry the widow of his deceased brother to raise up the family name (Deuteronomy 25:5; Matthew 22:23-28). God would use that law to put Ruth in the line from which King David came, as well as the Messiah, i.e., Jesus Christ.

The title "kinsman" is Hebrew *goel*, indicating the man was able to buy Ruth and Naomi out of bankruptcy—i.e., slavery—paying off their debt and setting them free. But the law required a second step. At the same time, he would marry the dead man's widow and reestablish the family name.

So we see the power of God working through a heathen young girl— Ruth—who is turning toward God. At the same time, we see the power of God working through a rich businessman who glorifies God—Boaz.

While Ruth was working, she caught Boaz's eye. Probably she worked as hard and diligent as any working girl in the field. Maybe she was not as well dressed or as flighty as the other young women. After all, Ruth was a widow with a dead husband back in Moab.

Probably, Boaz was in his 40s, while Ruth was in her late 20s. By today's standards they were not a young couple. But they were young enough that she could conceive and have a child.

When Boaz began asking the workers about Ruth, he found out she had worked hard, worked all morning, and had not taken a break/liberties with the food prepared for Boaz's workers.

Because she caught Boaz's eye, he invited her to have lunch with his workers, eating the cooked grain and drinking water from the jug.

To keep her around, Boaz said, "*Do not go to glean in another field, nor go from here, but stay close by my young women*" (Ruth 2:8). So, after the day was over Ruth took all the grain she had gathered from the field, put it in her large apron—or perhaps a sack—and took it home to Naomi. Then her mother-in-law saw it was more grain than she expected. It was then Ruth told Naomi, "*The man's name with whom I worked today is Boaz*" (Ruth 2:19).

That name, Boaz, was the spark that lit a fire in the heart and hope of Naomi. She recognized he was her relative. Naomi, who had no hope and no future, now had the motivation to make Boaz marry Ruth. So the motive in both the heart of Ruth and Boaz had entered the heart of Naomi.

THE END OF THE HARVEST

All the grain was brought into the threshing floor where the workers would use a long stick to thresh the grain, separating wheat kennels from its chaff or its husks. Once this was finished, there was usually a closing banquet, where Boaz would have a celebration dinner for all of his workers.

But Naomi directed Ruth differently. The elderly mother-in-law knew that Boaz would sleep that night on the threshing floor to protect his grain. After all, it had taken months to grow the grain, and the work of many people to harvest and separate the grain from the hulks. So he slept there to protect his cash crop.

Naomi knew all these facts, so she directed Ruth to go to the threshing floor under the cover of darkness. This was not an immoral act; she was not going to tempt him; nothing happened like that. When Boaz laid down to sleep, Ruth came to take the role of a servant. She slept at his feet such as a servant would do for the protection of his master. Also, the master would put his cold feet on the servant to keep them warm while he slept. Of course, the same covering was used for Boaz's feet and Ruth's body.

In the middle of the night Boaz was awakened and realized Ruth was lying at his feet. Boaz said, *"Who are you?"*

Ruth asked him to perform his family duty to her by paying/buying her out of slavery and bankruptcy. She said, *"Take your maidservant under your wing, for you are a close relative,"* i.e., *goel* (Ruth 3:9). That night Boaz agreed to redeem both Naomi and Ruth. He sent her home with a sack full of grain. As a matter of fact, there was so much grain that when Naomi saw it she counseled Ruth to be patient and trust God who was working. *"Sit still, my daughter...for the man will not rest until he has concluded the matter this day"* (Ruth 3:18).

Next Morning

Early in the morning, Boaz went to the city gate, the place where business was conducted for the city. All the businessmen would come there for buying, selling, and trading.

Boaz found the man who had the right to the property that had belonged to Elimelech and Naomi. Boaz negotiated to buy the property out of bankruptcy so he could own it. With it came the opportunity to marry Ruth and raise up the family line.

Many men would not fulfill their leviratical marriage responsibility. They did not want to continue the family line of someone else; they wanted to extend their own family line. And here was Boaz willing to give up his heritage and future recognition so he could fulfill the line of Elimelech.

Boaz paid off the mortgage and received legal rights belonging to Naomi and Ruth. He took Ruth as his wife, and they settled into living in his home.

Grandma Naomi

When Ruth and Boaz gave birth to their son, they turned to Grandma Naomi, giving her the most important task of her life—raising their son, Obed.

Ruth would have been busy managing the large household, which included servants in the house as well as servants in the field. The wife of a rich landowner had the responsibly to take care of the home, the meals, as well as the servants in the house and those who worked for her husband. Because of those pressing duties, Ruth needed some help from Naomi raising their son, Obed.

Interesting enough, the child is identified with his grandmother Naomi more than his mother Ruth. "*There is a son born to Naomi*" (Ruth 4:17). Even though Naomi was the grandmother, the people recognized that Ruth gave birth to Obed, but the son was from Naomi because Obed would carry on that family line.

The child Obed would become famous in Israel, not so much because of his mother or father, but because he became the grandfather of King David. "*Obed was the father of Jesse. Jesse was the father of David*" (Ruth 4:22, NLT). But greater than that, Ruth was listed in the line of the Messiah—Jesus Christ. "*Boaz begot Obed by Ruth, Obed begot Jesse, and Jesse begot David the king*" (Matthew 1:5).

Obed gave Naomi a purpose in life. She came back to Bethlehem with no hope. She told Ruth, "*Turn back, my daughters, go—for I am too old to have a husband. If I should say I have hope, if I should have a husband tonight and should also bear sons*" (Ruth 1:12).

When Obed was born, it was said of him, "*May he be to you a restorer of life*" (Ruth 4:15).

NAOMI'S NEW LIFE

- She had the respect of the town's women (Ruth 4:14-15).
- She had the love of her daughter-in-law (Ruth 4:15).
- She had restoration of hope and vision (Ruth 4:15).
- She had a grandson in the Messianic line (Ruth 4:16).

CHAPTER 3

ELIJAH FINISHED WELL

Did Elijah finish well? Yes! He finished as he lived. He was Elijah the Tishbite—the word *tish* means stranger or loner. Elijah seemed to always do things by himself. When we first see him, he announced three and half years of famine, then he ran to hide himself by the River Cherith beyond the Jordan. Today you would call it a forest; it is a wilderness to the west of the Jordan River. No one was with him except the ravens who fed him morning and evening.

Then Elijah went to Zarephath, a city in Sidon, outside the Promised Land. There he lived with a widow during the famine. He was fed daily by the hand of God who promised, *"The jar of flour will not be used up and the jug of oil will not run dry until the day the Lord sends rain on the land"* (1 Kings 17:14, ELT).

While most ministers of God sought an audience to deliver the message God gave them, Elijah left the crowd to seek solitude in the home of a widow.

When Elijah returned to his people in the Promised Land, he appeared on Mount Carmel where he stood alone against *"four hundred and fifty prophets of Baal, and the four hundred prophets of Asherah, who eat at Jezebel's table"* (1 Kings 18:19).

There a spiritual contest was fought between Elijah by himself, who stood against all the prophets of Baal. Elijah took control of the contest when he commanded, *"Get two bulls"* (1 Kings 18:23, ELT). They were told to secure the bulls for the sacrifice. Then Elijah announced, *"I will prepare the other bull and put it on the wood but not set fire to it"* (1 Kings 18:23, ELT).

There was no answer when the prophets of Baal prayed and begged their false gods for fire. Elijah stood alone all day until the evening hour. Then he alone prayed and God sent fire to consume his offering.

Then Elijah commanded, *"Seize the prophets of Baal. Don't let anyone get away!' They seized them, and Elijah had them brought down to the Kishon Valley and slaughtered there"* (1 Kings 18:40, ELT).

So what happened next? Elijah went to the top of Mount Carmel to pray to God alone. Then he finally saw *"a cloud as small as a man's hand is rising from the sea"* (1 Kings 18:44, ELT). He outran the chariot of Ahab returning to his home down Mount Carmel.

In his next major appearance, Elijah ended up hundreds of miles south of the Holy Land on Mount Sinai in the desert near the Red Sea. Again, Elijah the solitary one stood before God when he heard:

> *Then He* [God] *said, "Go out, and stand on the mountain before the Lord." And behold, the Lord passed by, and a great and strong wind tore into the mountains and broke the rocks in pieces before the Lord, but the Lord was not in the wind; and after the wind an earthquake, but the Lord was not in the earthquake; and after the earthquake a fire, but the Lord was not in the fire; and after the fire a still small voice* (1 Kings 19:11-12).

It was there God gave Elijah the commission to deliver to the kings of these nations.

ELIJAH ON HIS WAY TO THE FINISH LINE: 2 KINGS 2:1-10

After spending his life alone with God, Elijah was leaving the mountains of Judah, walking down to the Jordan River valley to cross the river and go to Heaven alone. The Bible introduces this scene: *"when the Lord was about to take up Elijah into heaven"* (2 Kings 2:1). It seems that everyone knew Elijah was going to go to Heaven (2 Kings 2:3, 5, 7). Even though everyone knew, only a few saw it take place (2 Kings 2:15). However, in spite of this knowledge, some did not think Elijah went to Heaven but they thought he went to a mountain and was hiding there (2 Kings 2:16-18).

As you look at Elijah's final day, note the progression from Gilgal down the mountain to Bethel. He continued on down the mountain to Jericho, then to Jordan, and he crossed the Jordan. There, Elijah went to Heaven. In each move of Elijah, he moved away from a nation of idols that provoked God. And where was he going? He was going to be with God. When you think about Elijah crossing the Jordan, remember throughout Scripture that crossing the Jordan is a symbol of passing through death into the presence of God.

Apparently there was a secret everyone knew about. *"A group of prophets from Bethel came to Elisha and asked him, 'Did you know that the Lord is going to take your master away from you today?'"* (2 Kings 2:3, ELT). Elisha answered, *"Of course I know. Be quiet about it"* (2 Kings 2:3, ELT).

As you look at this developing scene, Jordan was a well-known symbol of death. So Elijah was able to walk through death without harm. He took his robe to hit the water and the Jordan River parted, and Elijah crossed on dry land. Is this a picture of him walking through death without harm? Is it a prediction that believers who know Jesus Christ can walk through death without harm because we come out on the other side in the presence of God?

Next, there is a picture of a chariot taking Elijah to Heaven. Is this a picture of our future rapture that will take us to Heaven? Does this mean we can go to Heaven in a similar way that Elijah went to God's presence?

Yet in the midst of this developing scene, old Elijah continually said to young Elisha, *"stay here"* (2 Kings 2:6). Why was he saying that? Perhaps to test the faith of young Elisha. Perhaps Elijah was telling Elisha to stay back because he wanted to go to Heaven alone? Also, the old prophet told him to stay back because Elisha might be killed by the final scene. Perhaps he told him to stay back because he wanted to test his character and calling.

It was then that old Elijah said to young Elisha, *"Tell me what I can do for you before I am taken away"* (2 Kings 2:9, ELT). At this place the faith of young Elisha was sterling. He answered the question correctly, *"Please let a double portion of your spirit be upon me"* (2 Kings 2:9).

Young Elisha had faith to ask for a difficult thing. Apparently old Elijah recognized the difficulty of the request: *"If you see me when I am taken from you, it shall be so for you; but if not, it shall not be so"* (2 Kings 2:10).

They continued walking. Did they know how long they would be walking? Did they know where they were walking? Also, did they know why they were walking? *"As they were walking along and talking, suddenly a chariot of fire appeared, drawn by horses of fire. It drove between the two men, separating them, and Elijah was carried by a whirlwind into heaven"* (2 Kings 2:11, ELT).

When young Elisha was asking for a double portion of the spirit, for what was he asking? Was he asking for the inner character and determination of the old man? Did young Elisha want to have the strong will of old Elijah?

Perhaps Elisha was asking to have the influence of the older man. Everywhere Elijah went people knew about him; his reputation spread among the people of Israel. Did young Elisha want that reputation?

Perhaps young Elisha was asking for a double portion, referring to miracles. Old Elijah preformed seven miracle in his lifetime. God answered the prayer of young Elisha who had asked for a double portion. Young Elisha performed fourteen miracles.

When old Elijah said, "You have asked for a hard thing," why was it a hard request? No miracle is too hard for God, but did Elijah feel Elisha was asking for a miracle and this was a difficult (hard) thing? Perhaps old Elijah thought it would be hard for him to teach or give this lesson to a young man. Old Elijah knew how long it had taken him to learn all the lessons of walking with God. So old Elijah knew all the difficulties he had gone through to learn the lessons of God, and young Elisha would have to go through the same difficulties as he did. Therefore, it would be a "hard thing."

What was the response of young Elisha when the old man was whisked away by the chariot into Heaven? *"Elisha saw it and cried out, 'My father! My father! I see the chariots and charioteers of Israel!'* (2 Kings 2:12, NLT).

Who were these horses that pulled the chariots? Does God have horses in Heaven? And do some good horses go to Heaven when they die and some bad horses go to hell when they die? Probably not. The horses were probably angels who take us to Heaven when we die (Luke 16:22).

The word *fiery* means the same as *seraphim*, which is a description of the angels. *"God makes His angels flaming fire"* (Psalm 104:4, ELT). Therefore, fiery angels were pulling this chariot which Elijah rode in.

Be quick to notice that young Elisha was not whisked to Heaven with the old man. Only one went for a chariot ride— only Elijah. Just as Elijah was alone in serving God in life, he was alone riding alone to meet God. Elijah was a true Tishbite.

Young Elisha cried out, *"Where is the Lord God of Elijah?"* (2 Kings 2:14). That is an easy question to answer—God is in Heaven ruling over all things and controls the purpose of all things. God is where He has always been. But the question that should have been asked was, "Where are the Elijahs of the Lord God?" What we need today are more Elijahs. Not many people will walk with God—unquestionably serve God—so they can be taken to Heaven to be with God.

Today's Question Is: Where Are the Elijahs of the Lord God?

Notice what Elisha did after he asked that difficult question. *"He struck the water with Elijah's cloak"* (2 Kings 2:14, ELT). He went back across the Jordan.

And at the beginning of Elisha's ministry he was not alone. From a distance the "sons of the prophets" watched what was happening and exclaimed, *"Elijah's spirit rests upon Elisha!"* (2 Kings 2:15, ELT). They knew and ran out to meet him. Elisha was surrounded by the sons of the prophets. He was never alone but had witnesses with him.

These sons of the prophets had seen Elijah was taken away in a chariot. But they did not have the faith of their leader—they did not have the faith of Elisha. They asked, *"Just say the word and fifty of our strongest men will search the wilderness for your master. Perhaps the Spirit of the Lord has left him on some mountain or in some valley"* (2 Kings 2:16, ELT). Elisha told them not to go searching for the old man. But they did it anyway, and they could not find him. Why? Because Elijah was in Heaven with the Lord.

APPLICATIONS FOR FINISHING WELL

Life is more than faithfully running your race—it is important how you finish. God had tasks for Elijah to do, but Elijah finished well and God received him into Heaven. The sons of the prophets knew that, and they could spread the word everywhere, and in so doing the influence of Elijah continued beyond his trip to Heaven.

Learn from Elijah. After you spend your life walking with God and serving Him, then your finish in death should testify how you lived for God. Everyone should know you went to be with God and enjoy His presence.

Note that Elijah had a continuous battle with the kings, both in Judah and Israel. But in his last event, Elijah went out as a conqueror. God had a special finish for Elijah—God took him home in a chariot. One more thing, it is good that God did not answer all of Elijah's selfish prayers. Once Elijah prayed, *"Take my life"* (1 Kings 19:4). If you ever get discouraged and think about asking God to take your life, remember Elijah. God still had things for him to do on this earth, and He still has things for you to do on this earth.

So plan to finish to finish well!

CHAPTER 4

JOHN, 90 YEARS OLD, FINISHED WELL

I, John, both your brother and companion in the tribulation and kingdom and patience of Jesus Christ, was on the island that is called Patmos for the word of God and for the testimony of Jesus Christ. I was in the Spirit on the Lord's Day, and I heard behind me a loud voice, as of a trumpet…and when I saw Him, I fell at His feet as dead. But He laid His right hand on me, saying to me, "Do not be afraid; I am the First and the Last. I am He who lives, and was dead, and behold, I am alive forevermore. Amen. And I have the keys of Hades and of Death"
(Revelation 1:9–10, 17–18).

The apostle John finished well because he began well. He was numbered among the first disciples called to follow Jesus. *"Two disciples followed Jesus. Andrew first found his own brother and pointed him to Jesus. John also found his brother. 'We have found the Messiah, the Christ'"* (John 1:35-41, ELT).

Technically Andrew is the first called disciple, because he is clearly identified in the text as the first one called. The other disciple with him was John who did not identify himself as he wrote the gospel of John.

When compared to the twelve disciples, John was the youngest, probably around 17 years old when he began following Jesus. So how do we identify youthfulness? Young people are enthusiastic, so John enthusiastically, immediately began to follow Jesus. Second, youth are exploring, so following Jesus was a new experience in the life of John, for no one had ever followed God as He walked in human flesh. Also, John was self-centered as are most youth. They must learn humility and learn consideration for other people. The Bible describes John's youthfulness, calling him a "son of thunder" (Mark 3:17). Remember he was the one who forbade people to cast out demons (Luke 9:49-50).

John the impetuous disciple eventually became John the apostle of love when he was identified as loved by Jesus (John 13:23). Then he called himself *"the disciple whom Jesus loved"* (John 21:7). Later in life he was known as the apostle of love (1 John 4:7).

And what changed John from an impetuous youth to the apostle of love? Jesus changed him because he identified with Jesus when he leaned on Jesus' breast (John 13:25).

Also, John grew spiritually by taking responsibility when Jesus said, "Follow Me." He continued to do it throughout Jesus' life. As a matter of fact, at the last recorded event in John's gospel Jesus said to him, "Follow Me" (John 21:19).

No wonder John wrote, *"He who says he abides in Him ought himself also to walk just as He walked"* (1 John 2:6).

Then the expectation principle caused John to grow in moral character and love. Jesus expected much of John when He told the young disciple, *"Take care of my mother"* (John 19:25-27, ELT).

FOLLOWING WELL—FINISHING WELL

John began following Jesus when he was 17 years old and continued faithfully for three and half years while Jesus was on earth. Once Jesus went up into the mountain to pray, taking three disciples with Him—Peter, James, and John.

How did John finish well? One disciple betrayed Jesus—Judas Iscariot. Ten disciples ran away when Jesus was arrested and they did not come back to follow Him until after Jesus was resurrected from the dead. But John followed Jesus from His arrest in the garden of Gethsemane to the trial in the house of Caiaphas. Then he followed Jesus from the beatings in prison to the cross. When he realized Jesus was actually going to die, he left to go get Mary the mother of Jesus. John brought her to the cross. It was then Jesus gave John the commission to take care of His mother—Mary (John 19:25-27). At that point John took Jesus' mother to his own house.

On Resurrection Day—the first Easter—John was first at the tomb (John 20:2-4). A few weeks later when Jesus appeared to the fishermen on the Sea of Galilee, John was the first to recognize the resurrected Jesus (John 21:1-7). In the early church days when persecution broke out against believers, John remained in Jerusalem during those difficult times (John 8:1). Also, in the early church, John was among the first to recognize Paul as an apostle (Galatians 2:9).

Eventually John pastored and led the church in Ephesus. When I visited the ruins of Ephesus, the home of Mary, the mother of Jesus, was pointed out to me, suggesting it was there where she died. John left the cross with Jesus' mother and took care of her until she died. John was a faithful follower of Jesus who finished well.

John was eventually arrested and imprisoned on the isle of Patmos where he was held as a political prisoner. It was then John wrote the book of Revelation.

> *I, John, both your brother and companion in the tribulation and kingdom and patience of Jesus Christ, was on the island that is called Patmos for the word of God and for the testimony of Jesus Christ. ...I heard behind me a loud voice, as of a trumpet, saying, "...What you see, write in a book"*
>
> (Revelation 1:9–11).

FINISHING WELL IN JOHN'S 90S

John was an elderly man, approximately 90 years old when he was imprisoned in a cave on the isle of Patmos. It was a small island perhaps 8 by 10 miles in size. It was located in the Aegean Sea off the coast of Asia Minor (modern-day Turkey). John lived in a cave while a prisoner on Patmos. Today it is called the Cave of the Apocalypse.

I visited that cave on a Sunday morning during the summer of 2012, leading a class of approximately 20 Liberty University students studying the writings of John. As we entered the cave there were 18 worshipers in the first opening, being led in worship by Greek Orthodox Church leaders. We were told a group had met for worship continuously in that spot every Sunday since the first century AD. The cave walls were blackened with years of candle smoke and the walls were continuously damp. We were not able to interrupt their worship service, but they allowed us to walk around the edge of the room to the next two rooms, each approximately 10 by 10 feet. I tried to image where John would have slept on that cold, hard floor.

JOHN'S PROPHETIC VISION

John was writing the book of Revelation when God gave him a series of prophetic revelations, *"I heard behind me a loud voice. I turned to see One like the Son of Man"* (Revelation 1:10-13, ELT).

If you were taken into Heaven, what would you like to see? Streets of gold, your heavenly home, family and friends, the one who is responsible for your salvation—or would you want to see Jesus? When John was taken to Heaven, he saw Jesus, who told him, *"Do not be afraid; I am the First and the Last"* (Revelation 1:17).

John was given a commission by Jesus, *"I am He who lives, and was dead, and behold, I am alive forevermore. Amen. And I have the keys of Hades and of Death"* (Revelation 1:18). Then Jesus instructed, *"Write down what you have seen—both the things that are now happening and the things that will happen"* (Revelation 1:19, NLT).

John was ready to enter Heaven, *"I looked, and behold, a door standing open in heaven. And the first voice which I heard was like a trumpet speaking with me, saying, 'Come up here, and I will show...'"* (Revelation 4:1). Because John was so close to Jesus on earth, now the apostle wanted to be close to His side in Heaven. So it was only natural Jesus invited John to come up into Heaven so He could show the aged apostle around. Did Jesus point out John's eventual heavenly home?

While the apostle was writing at the end of the first century, he also saw many other things in this prophetic vision. He saw the second coming of Jesus Christ. *"I saw Heaven open and a white horse. Sitting on him was called Faithful and True; the armies in Heaven followed Him"* (Revelation 19:11, 14, ELT).

Can you imagine that over 2,000 years ago John saw the second coming of Jesus that would occur over two millennia in the future? Because Jesus is timeless and He surpasses time, He has always lived in yesterday, today, and forever. Jesus lifted John up so he could see the future.

The apostle John not only saw Jesus, but he saw his future home and the home of all believers, *"I saw a new heaven and a new earth, for the first heaven and the first earth had passed away"* (Revelation 21:1).

But John saw more than just the streets of Heaven. He saw mansions and the Tree of Life where fruit was growing that would always be ripe each month of the year. The leaves of the tree were for the healing of the nations. He also saw a pure crystal stream of water flowing out of the throne of God down the center of Heaven. There were streets on either side of the river.

But more than streets, rivers, and houses, John experienced the presence of God Himself. *"The tabernacle of God is with men, and He will dwell with them…. God Himself will be with them"* (Revelation 21:3).

Because John saw everything new, beautiful, and wonderful, he did not have to remember the past with all of its failures and disappointments. There was *"no more death, nor sorrow, nor crying. There shall be no more pain, for the former things have passed away"* (Revelation 21:4).

John saw the place where he would live when he died, and he would die shortly. John saw the conditions where he would spend eternity, and he would be there shortly. John saw the presence of God the Father, the One he had worshiped all his life, and he would be there shortly. John felt the warmth and comfort of the Holy Spirit who had taught him spiritual lessons and guided his writing of Scriptures. But most of all, John saw again Jesus Christ, his Master and Teacher on earth, and bowed in adoration before Him who saved and gave him eternal life.

PRINCIPLES LEARNED FROM JOHN

1. FINISH WELL BY IDENTIFYING WITH JESUS.

Pastoral leadership was transferred to Jesus' disciples as they ministered with Him and for Him. But the heart and soul of Jesus was transferred as He spent time with them. Young John became like Jesus, because it seems Jesus spent more time with him than any other. John included in his narration leaning on Jesus' breast at the Last Supper (John 13:23-25).

2. LOVE DEFINED.

Youthful love is described as "love-receiving." While immaturity seeks the feeling of love, those who experience the love of Jesus learn *love-giving*. John learn spiritual lessons of *love-giving*, and as an old man wrote perhaps the best definition of love, "*Greater love has no one than this, than to lay down one's life for his friends*" (John 15:13).

3. FORGIVENESS MAKES YOU LOVE.

Remember John made several mistakes as a youth. He condemned the Samaritans and was quick to judge others. However, he was forgiven by Jesus Christ and that gave new direction to his life. Therefore, as an elderly disciple, he was known as "the apostle of love." He identified himself, "*Beloved, let us love one another, for love is of God; and everyone who loves is born of God and knows God*" (1 John 4:7).

The greatness of our forgiveness reflects the depth of our love for God. God has done all He can to forgive our sins; now it is up to us to understand His forgiveness, explore the meaning of His forgiveness, receive His forgiveness, and worship Him because of forgiveness.

4. THE RESPONSIBILITY OF GROWTH PRINCIPLE.

Many have experienced sin in this life, and because of sin they are not growing. However, the secret of spiritual growth is based on your understanding of Jesus, His truth, and what He has done for you. "*He who says he abides in Him ought himself also to walk just as He walked*" (1 John 2:6).

5. LOVE MAKES YOU "OTHERS" CONSCIOUS.

Jesus began His ministry with people, not with programs, not by spending time with multitudes, not by preaching sermons, not even by doing miracles. People were the most important aspect of Jesus' life. Remember to be as influential as Jesus, a disciple-maker must invest his life in followers. To reach the world, Jesus influenced individuals who were others-motivated.

6. THE GREATEST ATTRIBUTE YOU CAN HAVE IN LIFE IS SELF-CONTROL.

Until you can control yourself, you cannot control your talents, attitudes, or even your desires. A person is weak when he is controlled by his emotions. Also a person who is controlled by his vision is superficial if he does not have self-discipline to work to accomplish his vision. It seems young John originally sought self-exhortation, but the more time he spent with Jesus, the more he learned the strength of *love-giving*, which comes from *love-receiving*.

7. THE HEARER-SEER PRINCIPLE.

Before you can be a great learner, you must be a great seer. Those who are great seers understand what they see and then apply it to their lives. John applied the principle of hearing/seeing and was called the "seer" for Jesus Christ (1 John 1:1; Revelation 1:9-18).

8. THE LOVE EXPECTATION PRINCIPLE.

How does God motivate His people? By telling them what He expects of their personal life and what He expects of them in ministry/service. Did

Jesus expect much of John? Yes. Jesus gave John one of the most important responsibilities—Jesus gave John the responsibly of caring for His mother, Mary, after He died. Because Jesus was the oldest of her sons, it was His responsibility to take care of His mother in her old age. So Jesus asked John to take care of His mother. Jesus looked beyond John's youthful outlook and motived the young man to excellence.

9. FAITHFUL LOVE LEADS YOU TO BECOME A FOLLOWER.

Because Jesus loved John, the young disciple followed Jesus everywhere, all the time, for all of his life. When we learn Jesus' love for us, we will also follow Him, all the time, for all of our life.

CHAPTER 5

PAUL FINISHED WHAT HE FIRST BEGAN

Paul did not start off serving the Lord very well; it was all about keeping the law and not about his love for the Lord. "*I [Paul] was circumcised when I was eight days old. I am a pure-blooded citizen of Israel...I was a member of the Pharisees, who demand the strictest obedience to the Jewish law*" (Philippians 3:5, NLT). While keeping the law was his first expectation, everything changed when he met Jesus Christ. He was born again when Jesus appeared to him on the road to Damascus. He no longer served the law, he became a servant of the Lord, Jesus Christ. He had a new motivation for his life: "*For me, to live is Christ*" (Philippians 1:21). He had a new power in his life: "*I can do all things through Christ who strengthens me*" (Philippians 4:13).

When Paul met Jesus Christ, everything changed. His new purpose was to know Jesus Christ, his new power was the indwelling Holy Spirit, and he enjoyed the presence of Jesus Christ who controlled his life. His new passion was to carry out the Great Commission, preaching the gospel to everyone in the world.

When people say everything in Paul's life changed—not really. Paul's passion did not change. He served the law tirelessly and sacrificially; now he served Jesus Christ with the same recklessness. Just as he tried to conform himself to the strict standards of the Old Testament law, now he made every attempt to conform his character and love into the image of Jesus Christ.

PAUL'S PASSION

Paul had a threefold passion that drove him in all that he did. First, he wanted to complete/finish the Great Commission in his lifetime. Second, he wanted his inner life to be conformed to the likeness of Jesus Christ. Third, he wanted to serve Christ faithfully to his death or rapture, whichever came first.

COMPLETING THE GREAT COMMISSION

The Great Commission was given by Jesus Christ on five different occasions; each time Jesus emphasized a different aspect of the Great Commission.

No one questions the command of the Great Commission to go and win lost people to Jesus Christ. But many miss the second aspect of the Great Commission, i.e., planting New Testament churches. This means reaching lost people in every culture of the world.

The command in Matthew 28:19 includes discipling "all the nations" or peoples. Mark 16:15 incudes the entire world as the sphere and every creature (person) as the goal for the proclamation of the gospel. Luke 24:47-48 directs us to preach the message of Christ's offer of forgiveness for sins to be taken into all the nations of the world beginning at Jerusalem; and John 20:21 promises spiritual power to those who are sent. Acts 1:8 teaches that, when filled with the Holy Spirit, believers are to be witnesses about the facts of salvation to the most remote points of the earth.

The Great Commission was given at five different times in separate locations. On each occasion the Lord added to the previous command, and the reader must see the total picture to understand the full implications of the Great Commission.

PAUL COMPLETING THE GREAT COMMISSION

The Great Commission can be summarized in four great goals: 1) no individual person left out, 2) no people group left out, 3) no geographical place left out, 4) no language group left out. These fourfold,

WHERE	WHEN	TO WHOM	WHAT	KEY	
1.	John 20:21	Upper Room Jerusalem	Resurrection	10 disciples	I am sending you to go	Commission
2.	Mark 16:15	Upper Room Jerusalem	One week later	11 disciples	Go to all places in the world and preach to every person	Recipient
3.	Matthew 28:19-20	Mountain in Galilee	At least two weeks	11 disciples	Disciple all people groups then baptize and teach	Strategy
4.	Luke 24:46-48	Jerusalem	40th day	11 disciples	Preach repentance and forgiveness of sins based on resurrection of Christ	Content
5.	Acts 1:8	Mount of Olives	40th day	11 disciples	Jerusalem to uttermost parts of the earth	Geography

all-encompassing commands took hold of Paul's life and directed all that he was and would accomplish in life.

1. NO PERSON LEFT OUT.

Because Jesus died for the world, God wants everyone to repent (2 Peter 3:9). God wants salvation preached to everyone so they will call upon the name of Jesus so their sins will be forgiven. Throughout Paul's ministry, he spent his life attempting to take the gospel to everyone within reach/hearing/communication.

The above verse, 2 Peter 3:9, focuses on repentance. That is the first step a lost person takes when turning from sin to reach out to Jesus Christ in faith for salvation. How do you know a person is really reaching out to God? When he lets go (repents) of sin that has easily enslaved him.

2. NO PEOPLE GROUP LEFT OUT.

The Great Commission explicitly targets preaching the gospel to every culture: *"Go make disciples of every [ethna] people group"* (Matthew 28:19, ELT). God focuses on culture because it has the presence and power that influences/shapes an individual personality/response to life. When we preach in every culture, we can focus a lost person's attention on Jesus Christ, which will lead to salvation.

The power/influence of culture was introduced at the tower of Baal (Genesis 11:1-11). God confused the languages of the people and their ability to communicate with each other in their cooperate personality/culture in which they lived. God changed their communication/culture so they would spread out over the face of the earth. Therefore, God knows culture, loves culture, and wants everyone reached in every culture. So when the gospel is preached to them, they can be saved within their culture.

3. NO PLACE LEFT OUT.

Paul gave us geographical direction: *"to preach the Good News where the name of Christ has never been heard"* (Romans 15:20, NLT). Because people live everywhere, God wants us to go everywhere with the gospel so we can reach everyone with the message of Jesus Christ.

Years ago, I was on an evangelistic outreach mission trip with the teenagers from Kansas City Baptist Temple, Kansas, and we were about 20 miles outside of Tijuana, Mexico. The church bus had taken around 20 high school students for a day of evangelism going from one small town to another in the desert area outside Tijuana. The young people were visiting every house and leaving a gospel tract in Spanish. A few teenagers could speak Spanish, so they explained the gospel. It was 5:00 p.m. and all wanted to go back to the camping area. Roscoe Brewer, the missions director at the church said, "Hey gang, there is one more village that needs the gospel. We have never been to that village; we need to give a tract to everyone there." The students began to complain about being tired and wanted to go and get cleaned up to wash off the heat; and of course, they were hungry. It was then Roscoe pleaded, "There may be people in this village who will never hear the gospel and will go to hell if we don't reach them. Please, gang, let's go to their town to reach one last person for Jesus Christ." I have never forgotten Roscoe's passion, and we went to the town to pass out tracts to everyone.

4. No language left out.

As we go into all the world, we must not only recognize different cultures, but we must reach people in their different languages. *"This message should be proclaimed...to all people groups"* (Luke 24:47, ELT). Not only must we go to the people to tell them about Jesus Christ, but we must also tell them in their own language so they can understand the gospel and be saved. That is why missionaries spend a good part of their preparation learning both a language and the culture. Then they go to the mission field to preach the gospel to everyone.

5. Paul's personal commitment.

The above four commitments taught in the Word of God weigh heavily upon every Christian today. But beyond that, Paul had his own personal commitment of what he must do to take the gospel to everyone. *"I have been following the plan...those who have never been told about him will see, those who have never heard of him will understand"* (Romans 15:21, NLT).

TO BE CONFORMED TO THE IMAGE OF JESUS CHRIST

Beyond the passion of reaching everyone, Paul also had a passion to be personally conformed to the image of Jesus Christ. Not outwardly only, but inwardly. It was Paul's desire to grow daily in Christ, and that involved putting to death any lust or wrong desire when he said, *"I die daily"* (1 Corinthians 15:31).

But more than just a daily giving up sin and yielding self to God, Paul spoke about a once and for all commitment of his life to Jesus Christ when he said he was first saved. *"I have been crucified with Christ; it is no longer I who live, but Christ lives in me; and the life which I now live in the flesh I live by faith in the Son of God, who loved me and gave Himself for me"* (Galatians 2:20).

Paul had a passion to know Christ intimately not only in a one-time salvation experience, but also on a moment-by-moment basis. His desire: *"I want to know Christ and experience the mighty power that raised him from the dead. I want to suffer with him, sharing in his death, so that one way or another I will experience the resurrection from the dead!"* (Philippians 3:10-11, NLT).

Paul wanted to be daily conformed into the image of Jesus Christ. *"I focus on this one thing: Forgetting the past and looking forward to what lies ahead, I press on to reach the end of the race and receive the heavenly prize for which God, through Christ Jesus, is calling us"* (Philippians 3:13-14, NLT). This book is about *Finishing Well*—did you see that Paul wanted to finish his race well?

TO SERVE FAITHFULLY TO HIS DEATH

Paul had several attempts by the enemy to murder him, plus many other dangers he faced. He testified, *"In everything we do, we show that we are true ministers of God. We patiently endure troubles and hardships and calamities of every kind. We have been beaten, been put in prison, faced angry mobs, worked to exhaustion, endured sleepless nights, and gone without food"* (2 Corinthians 6:4-5, NLT).

Yet when Paul was in prison in Rome and facing death he testified, *"You know how much persecution and suffering I have endured. You know all about how I was persecuted in Antioch, Iconium, and Lystra—but the Lord rescued me from all of it"* (2 Timothy 3:11, NLT).

Paul testified he would *finish well* his life's race. *"I have fought the good fight, I have finished the race, and I have remained faithful. And now the prize awaits me—the crown of righteousness, which the Lord, the righteous Judge, will give me on the day of his return. And the prize is not just for me but for all who eagerly look forward to his appearing"* (2 Timothy 4:7-8, NLT).

Tradition tells us that Paul died on a flaming cross in Nero's garden. He was covered in oil and burned to death for the sake of Jesus Christ.

Paul died physically in Rome, but remember he died spiritually when he originally surrendered his life to Jesus Christ. Then, Paul died daily each time he surrendered his will to do the task given him by Jesus Christ. Then ultimately Paul died a martyr's death for Jesus Christ. He wrote:

> *My life has already been poured out as an offering to God. The time of my death is near. I have fought the good fight, I have finished the race, and I have remained faithful. And now the prize awaits me—the crown of righteousness, which the Lord, the righteous Judge, will give me on the day of his return. And the prize is not just for me but for all who eagerly look forward to his appearing* (2 Timothy 4:6-8, NLT).

Paul *finished well*!

CHAPTER 6

YOUR TIME TO FINISH WELL

If someone asked, "Will you finish well?" how would you answer? Is it about your stamina—do you have enough strength to finish? Or is it about conditions—will the race get rained out? Or snowed out? Or is it too hot? Too cold to finish?

Probably the question would involve time—do you have enough time to finish well? How long will it take to finish well? If you run out of time, will you finish poorly or not finish at all?

MEASURING TIME TO FINISH WELL

We all have been entered into the race of life. We all are running on the racetrack of our home, school, work, or neighborhood where we live. We all face competitors—some we will beat, others we won't. Like it or not, our race has begun, and everyone around us is running. We had a starting line—birth—and there is a finish line—death. We all are on the clock.

We all have been given the gift of time. Like money, use it well. Like stocks or bonds, guard it well. Like health, nourish it so it will nourish you. Use your time wisely, profitably, and prayerfully, and you can *finish well*.

What is the meaning of time? When we ask the question, "What time is it?" we never think of the nature of time, only the appointment we need to make or the remaining time we have left until the next meeting.

Time is the continued sequence of existence or events in your life that comes as an irreversible succession from the past to the present to your future.

That is a technical definition of time, however. There are many other definitions of time. The everyday definition of time is what we see on the clock.

Another definition of time is a measurement of distance between events that happened in the past to the present and on to future. Time can be measured forward and backward.

Another definition of time is the mathematical tool for organizing the sequence of events.

Another definition of time is measuring the flow of events. Just as an hourglass measures the amount of sand flowing from the top to the bottom of the glass, so time is a continual flow of people and events of past history to the future.

The English word *clock* comes from the Dutch *kalocke,* which means bell. A bell was rung on sailing vessels to reflect the passage of hours, marked by the ringing of the bell designating the present time. Later, bells were used in abbeys for the people in the town to know the present time.

Historically, time was measured by gravity—the use of weights in a clock, like a grandfather clock. Over a period of years, clocks used a spring that would eventually wind down. Then, time was measured electronically. First by plugging into a wall socket. Then batteries powered clocks and wristwatches. Today, time is measured by atomic clocks that probe with microwaves, determining the frequency of vibrations to measure time more actually than any electric device. It probes the energy or movement of caesium atoms that have a total of 9,192,631,770 cycles in a second. Technically, the atomic clock can measure the distance between two spinning electrons.

God knew all these technical aspects when He created time. *"In the beginning God created the heavens and the earth"* (Genesis 1:1).

It is hard for the human mind to conceive, but there was a time when there was no such thing as time. There was only eternity and only God existed. But in an instant, God created the idea/concept of time, then gave it existence. We humans are still trying to understand and measure the time that God has given to us.

WHAT DOES TIME MEAN TO US?

Each person is given a short period of time to live on this earth. James asked the question, "*What is your life? It is even a vapor that appears for a little time and then vanishes away*" (James 4:14). Ah! Time is life—or we could say life is time.

From James' perspective, he tells us that whatever time is, it is temporary. However you define time, it is here and will disappear. As a matter of fact, the time it took me to write this chapter is finished and gone. That time will never come back.

Moses examined the shortness of a man's life when he said, "[People] *are like grass that springs up in the morning...it blooms and flourishes, but by evening it is dry and withered*" (Psalm 90:5-6, NLT). Time is here, then gone.

So our life is short according to God and Moses. How short? The Bible suggests, "*Seventy years are given to us! Some even live to eighty. But even the best years are filled with pain and trouble; soon they disappear, and we fly away*" (Psalm 90:10, NLT).

One sure thing about time—it will keep going, and eventually all people will die. Again Moses described time, "*Lord, through all the generations you have been our home! Before the mountains were created, before the earth was formed, you are God without beginning or end. You speak, and man turns back to dust* [they die]" (Psalm 90:1-3, TLB).

What was Moses trying to tell us? "*It is appointed for men* [and women] *to die once*" (Hebrews 9:27).

So we are born in time, we are captive to the sequence of time, and eventually our time on earth is finished and we die. But remember, God is greater than time. The greatest thing you can say about God is that He is not limited by time. "*A thousand years are but as yesterday to you! They are like a single hour!*" (Psalm 90:4, TLB).

THEREFORE, DON'T COUNT TIME—MAKE TIME COUNT!

Everyone has been given the gift of time, including you. How many years, months, days, and seconds do you have left? No one knows; only God knows.

People often ask me how I get so much done. I don't have any more time than anyone else. But I try to get more done in the same amount of time. I try not to waste time, because I know once I waste it I will never get it back. I have tried to learn to make my time count. I believe what God says, "*Teach us to number our days, that we may gain a heart of wisdom*" (Psalm 90:12).

So what does "number our days" mean? It is more than counting seconds, minutes, hours, days, weeks, months, and years. When you double what you do in a day, you make that time count for eternity.

Count your days! Why? Because you are given a certain amount of time to begin with. You have not exhausted your time yet. And you don't have that much time left.

There are 365 days in a year. If you live to be 70 years old, you have lived 25,550 days. Once I had the privilege—a tearful and grieving responsibility—to preach the funeral of a two-year-old baby girl. I assured the family the little girl was in the presence of God. I told the story of a baby boy born to David and Bathsheba. The baby died, and of course David grieved over his death. However, David said, "*But now he is dead...can I bring him back again? I shall go to him, but he shall not return to me*" (2 Samuel 12:23).

David had the assurance that his little boy was in the presence of God where he would stand one day. In that funeral I gave the parents the assurance that one day they would be in the presence of God with their little baby girl.

When you think of counting your days, think of the little boy who does not have much money. He will always count his money. Why? Because he wants to see how much he has, what he can do with what he has, and how he can get the most out of the little bit of money he has left. Treat your days as the little boy treats his money.

Count your days because they go by quickly. And you never know what day will be your last day.

When I was a boy in school, it seemed like it took forever for recess to come. I would sit at my desk, many times not paying attention, but planning what I would do at recess. I thought about lunch and what I would eat and drink. Then I thought about my buddies and how we would play tag or some other game. When I was waiting for recess, time dragged slowly. When you were a child time seemed endless.

But the older you get, the faster time speeds by. Now when a week goes by, I ask, "Where did all the time go? And when a year goes by, I ask the same question, "Where did this year go?"

Remember, Moses said our time is, *"carried away like a flood"* (Psalm 90:5, ELT). Over the last 50 years I have seen floods rampage through the James River here in Lynchburg, Virginia. Floods come quickly and seem to disappear in a day or two. Our time is like the raging floods of the James River, where there was energy, power, and destruction. Finally, the James River rushed on, sweeping away everything in its path. Your life and your time is like a James River flood. When your life is gone, you will have the memories of life's flood, but also you have its aftermath.

MEASURE YOUR TIME BECAUSE YOU DO NOT GET A SECOND CHANCE

We all wish we had more time to pray and more time to spend in God's Word. So when the Bible tells us to "number our days," it means we ought to plan the amount of time we are going to spend in prayer, as well as how much time we are going to spend in the Word of God. We all wish we had more time to read the Bible, to do the work of God, to share Christ with the lost, to pray. So number your days, i.e., plan your time to do those activities for God.

Number your days you have left at work, at leisure, at eating, and even sleeping. You will find you really have had very little time invested in God. So number your days to make time for reading your Bible, prayer, meditation, the work of God, and worship.

The Average Week

- Fifty-two hours sleeping
- Fifty-six hours working and commuting
- Eight hours eating
- Twenty-four hours watching television and listening to music
- Sixteen hours non-scheduled time

Time Can Only Be Used Once

When you purchase something that can only be used once, it becomes more valuable to you until you use it. As a matter of fact, the greatest value that thing has is when you actually use it. So think of time as a purchased, valued commodity. You can only use it once. However, we wrongly think of time as something we can use over and over and over and over. So when we don't count our time, we don't think it is very valuable. What is time? It is like your first kiss—you can enjoy it only once. Time is like a fresh towel after a bath.

Remember, time is valuable! When you use something only once, it has much more value to you than anything you constantly use day after day. Think of a gift certificate at a restaurant that can only be used once. You enjoy the meal as well as the memory of the one who gave you the gift certificate.

Think of time as an opportunity to visit a place you have always wanted to see. When the opportunity comes, you actually get to walk through the museum, or visit the capital building, or visit the birthplace of a great president. Since you can only visit it once, make the most of your time and see all you can, learn all you can, and remember as much as possible.

Why count your time? There are 1,440 minutes in a day, and once you use each minute in the day, you cannot use them again.

There is a big difference between wasting time and learning time. That means there is a difference between wasting time and leisure time. Also, there is a difference between wasting time and waiting time. How do you define wasting time? It is a period when you could do something valuable and constructive, but you choose not to do it. Wasting time is wasting an opportunity that you will never have again. Wasting time is wasting your assets, energy, and mind. Wasting time is wasting the challenge of serving the Lord when given the opportunity. It is the challenge of meditating on God, and it is the renewal you get from reading His Scriptures.

So what can you do when you are waiting? You can plan, meditate, pray about what you do next—there are many things you can do when waiting. Learn to invest your time to enrich your life, and use all your time for the glory of God.

Let's not be so much of a busybody that we think we must be busy all the time. Sometimes when you are waiting, a little snooze may do you good. Maybe you get the needed physical strength for the next challenge or opportunity ahead. Sleeping is not wasting time; it is an investment to gain energy and to replenish your emotions and be ready for the next challenge and the next day. God built the human body to have rest and sleep, all to rejuvenate yourself. However, if you oversleep and spend too much time sleeping, you are wasting time.

INVESTING YOUR TIME IS FINISHING WELL

Don't think of counting time as wasting time. Think of counting time as an investment in something, as an investment in the future. Remember, spent money is like spent time—you don't see it again. But when you invest your money, it comes back to you in the future, and many times with interest. So if you can invest your time in doing profitable things—learning, evaluating, planning—time will come back to you with interest.

Jesus told us, *"Beware! Guard against every kind of greed. Life is not measured by how much you own"* (Luke 12:15, NLT). Yes, we invest our money to get interest back, or we invest our money to get a needed item to help us in life, or we invest our money to get an education, experience, or advancement.

While we invest our money to get interest back, we invest our time for different reasons. We are not investing our time to get money, but we want to live better, think better, work better, and do more for God. We invest our time to expand our contribution to the kingdom of God and to glorify God.

There was man sitting on death row in prison, waiting for the time when he was going to be executed for his crime. The man had appealed to the governor for clemency or a pardon; he did not want to die for his crime.

"Good news," the guard came to tell him. The prisoner thought the good news was a pardon or at least a stay of execution. But that was not the message.

The guard told the prisoner his uncle had died and left him with millions of dollars. The condemned prisoner was now a millionaire. But what good is being a millionaire if you have no time to use it, and death is staring you in the face?

All of us are like that prisoner. We are scheduled to die—some sooner, some later. Not an uncle, but our heavenly Father has given us our spiritual inheritance with all the happiness we could ever want. Your heavenly Father has given you time to live. He has given you this day, this moment. Now enjoy His spiritual heritage knowing that one day you will die.

To live in this life is ultimately to have some pain and suffering. When Adam and Eve sinned against God, they were promised two things. First, that Adam and his posterity would have to work by the sweat of their brow to earn a living. To the woman, God promised pain in childbirth (Genesis 3:16-19). And we have the legacy of Adam and Eve. Because we are born in sin, we will go through suffering in this life here on earth, and eventually we will die. Like it or not, all of us will get sick, some sicker than others, and all of us will die, and some sooner than others.

When you have good health, invest your time and energy in the work of God. Why? Because there may be days with bad health and limited time in the future. In the future you may be extremely limited in what you can do for God and how you can be used of God. Remember Paul's exhortation, "*For our present troubles are small and won't last very long. Yet they produce for us a glory that vastly outweighs them and will last forever!*" (2 Corinthians 4:17, NLT).

The apostle Paul had the calling of God upon his life and a challenge to reach the world with the gospel. Yet Paul had his moments of suffering and setback. Yes, even Paul had setbacks—a thorn in his flesh (2 Corinthians 12:7).

So today, if you don't have sufferings and afflictions, you can serve God effectively and happily. While some have to serve God through suffering and others serve God with limitations, you can serve God in good health, with a good mind, and good energy. Since we all eventually will suffer and die, let's number our days for the glory of God. Let's make our remaining days count for God.

While numbering your days, remember that you may have only a few days left, and when you do that, remember your afflictions are not nearly as bad as many other people who are suffering terribly. Rejoice in your life's suffering, because there may come a time when your sufferings will be worse.

But also remember, Heaven will be a much better place to live than what you have here on this earth. So number your days, and make your remaining time on earth count for eternity.

WHAT HAPPENS IF YOU WASTE TIME?

If you don't use your time properly, it will escape and get away from you.

If you don't count your days, you will get little done. There is a problem with time—it passes so quickly, and eventually the end will come! If you don't use your time wisely, you will lose it. That is where we get the old phrase, "Use it or lose it."

Oftentimes, I have to lead/preach a funeral for someone who has been a friend. As I look over the details of the deceased, I want to give the appropriate eulogy during the service. When you think about it, it is sad that you can tell almost every great thing a person has done in their life in less than ten minutes. I only have a few minutes to tell the people attending a funeral all the great things the deceased had accomplished in life. If you don't number your days, you will not accomplish much in life.

If you don't count your days now, it will get more difficult to count them with the passing of time. Remember, the natural inclination of the body is seeking rest, relief from pain, and avoidance of hard work. So what does that mean? It takes mental effort and physical discipline to force our body to work, work continually, and be productive. That is based on the premise that the human nature tends to be lazy. Therefore, we must "number our days." That means we must plan to use our days profitably, plan to be productive, plan to leave a legacy, plan to glorify God.

Years ago, I heard an audiotape of a pastor talking about "pay now and play later." He advised the young person to work hard the first part of his life so he could have some enjoyment and play time in the second half of his life. The speaker went on to point out that the young person who "plays first" will "pay later."

If in your 20s and 30s you spend all your time in play, and you don't learn a trade, you don't put money away for the future, you don't get the most out of your young physical body, you don't plan to invest your money for the future—you will pay later. Those who don't work hard in the first part of their life will pay in the last part of their life. However, those who spend their young life praying and investing their life for the future will enjoy the future.

There was a man in Virginia who spent his life sitting on the front porch of his house, waving at cars as they passed by. He was asked why. He answered, "Waving at people makes me happy." Then the questioner asked, "Well then, what else do you accomplish?" The man replied, "Nothing else...just making people happy." That man spent his life making himself and other people happy.

If you don't count your days, you dishonor God.

When you make your time count, you recognize that God is the author of time who created time and has given you a certain amount of time to use for His glory and purpose. *In the beginning God created the heavens and the earth*" (Genesis 1:1). In that creative act, God created time. At the beginning we defined time as "the distance between events." But in eternity past, there were no events; there was only God. But God who existed by Himself created the heavens with the planets and sun. So in the beginning, God created the heavens and the earth that began time. Now since the clock is ticking on the earth, your clock is ticking. Are you spiritually ready to die? Why not? Do you know when you will die? Of course not! Do you know how and when you will die? No! What are you going to do?

You should number your days to recognize God as the Creator of time, and He has given you time. But if you don't treat time properly, you don't properly honor God. Become a good steward of your time, managing your time for God and His glory.

We all hold the "deposit slip" of time that God has given to us. We are responsible to properly use our body, mind, emotions, and choices for the glory of God. A steward is a manager who manages money, resources, and time for another. Therefore, be a proper steward or proper manager of your time, talent, and treasure for the glory of God. And it all begins by properly managing your time as a good steward for God.

CONCLUSION

For the light makes everything visible. This is why it is said, "Awake, O sleeper, rise up from the dead, and Christ will give you light." So be careful how you live. Don't live like fools, but like those who are wise. Make the most of every opportunity in these evil days (Ephesians 5:14-16, NLT).

We have little time left before Jesus returns to earth or we die to go meet God. Therefore, honor God by honoring your time. Recognize all the advantages and privileges of your past time, thank God for your present existence, then commit your future time to God. Remember—your time is your life.

Epilogue

Not Finished—Life Continues After Death

Many people come to their time to die, then they go home to meet God. Their life is over, but did they *finish well*?

Your life is not measured by the length of time from your conception/birth to your death. No, not at all. Your life is measured past your death because your influence continues after you die. How you live before you die—and how you invest your life for God before you die—will have an influence after your physical life is gone.

You *finish well* when you leave a living legacy—your testimony continues to live, your influence continues its work, the purpose God gave you in life continues after you are gone. To *finish well* is to continue living throughout eternity, finishing what you began on earth.

Finishing well is not a final act; you still are influential on the stage of life. *Finishing well* is not a concluding statement; you will continue speaking into the life of your family, friends, and the world. *Finishing well* is not the ending—no, not at all. You finish well when God continues to use you in death as He used you in life.

For you, *finishing well* is entrance into God's presence to receive God's reward for a life well lived. *Finishing well* means beginning eternity, entering God's presence to worship Him forever, just as you worshiped and praised Him here on earth. To *finish well* means beginning eternity well.

Are you ready to finish and begin? Are you ready to live with God?

DAILY DEVOTIONS

DAY 01

BEGAN POORLY BUT FINISHED WELL

By faith Jacob, when he was dying, blessed each of the sons of Joseph, and worshiped, leaning on the top of his staff

(Hebrews 11:21).

The early life of Jacob tells you he did not begin well. He used deception and trickery to get the inheritance and family blessing from his older brother Esau. He use the same deception when working for Laban, his father-in-law. Yet he finished well God's vision and calling on his life (Genesis 28:12-22). Jacob is an inspiration to many who begin life poorly. The grace of God extends to the unlikely and transforms a poor beginning into a life blessed and used by God. That means everyone can be used by God and can be a living example of *"yet not I, but Christ"* (Galatians 2:20, KJV).

> *Lord, thank You for looking beyond the weakness and failings of Jacob to use him in Your ministry. Thank You for the encouragement that You can use me. Forgive me, lift me up, fill me with Your grace and power, use me in Your service. Amen.*

We see compromises when we look at Jacob halfway through his adult life. Add to that deception and selfish plans and acts. Yet God looked beyond his surface to see Jacob's heart. We see the grace of God when

Jacob looked beyond his sons to bless his grandsons. We serve a God who judges/rewards His servants on their whole life—not just how they began.

> *Thank You, Lord, for Your mercy that looked beyond Jacob's human frailties and even forgave his youthful blunders. Thank You for Your patience with me, thank You for Your forgiveness, and thank You for using me. Amen.*

Read: Genesis 28:1-22

DAY 02

FAMILY HATRED

From that time on, Esau hated Jacob because their father had given Jacob the blessing. And Esau began to scheme: "I will soon be mourning my father's death. Then I will kill my brother, Jacob"

(Genesis 27:41, NLT).

Yes, there is much love among physical family members, but there is also the possibility of deep hatred. In today's Scripture, "Esau hated Jacob" because Jacob had tricked his brother Esau out of the family inheritance and family money. Esau's hatred was so deep he planned, "I will kill my brother Jacob." You cannot properly understand Bible characters unless you realize they all had deceitful hearts, i.e., a sinful nature (Jeremiah 17:9; Romans 3:1-23). They did good things out of their new nature, but they also were deceitful and evil because of their old nature (Ephesians 4:28-31).

Lord, I have a sinful nature that tempts me to sin. Forgive me of both my sinful acts and sinful desires. Thank You for my new nature that promotes me to do and say the right things. Give me strength to follow my new nature and glorify You. Amen.

We see Jacob's old nature controlling his actions, and at times we see his new nature taking over. We learn that our heroes in the Bible are just like us. Let's learn preventative measures to block our old nature, and let's encourage our new nature to guide us into actions that please the Lord.

Lord, give me eyes to see the mistakes Jacob made—the same kinds of mistakes I might make. Give me a spiritual heart to understand my desires—both good and evil. Then give me courage to follow Your teachings and determination to keep doing right things. Amen.

Read: 1 Peter 1:3-25

DAY 03

WHY GOD CHOOSES

Then Israel [Jacob] *stretched out his right hand and laid it on Ephraim's head, who was the younger. "…His* [Manasseh's] *younger brother shall be greater than he"*

(Genesis 48:14, 19).

God established a principle early on to choose and bless the second born. Note God's blessing on second-born Abel, not Cain. Also, His blessing on second-born Isaac and not Ishmael. Then we look at God choosing Jacob over Esau. Remember, the blessing was not in the quality or character of the second born. God did not choose them because they were special—no! They became special because God choose them. Therefore, look beyond the men mentioned above. Their greatness is God's presence in their life. It was God's grace to overlook their weakness, and it was God's mercy that looked beyond their birth order to magnify His power and glory.

> *Lord, thank You for overlooking my weaknesses and faults, yet You have chosen me to follow You, serve You, and most of all to glorify You. There is nothing in me that deserves Your choice; it is all Your grace. Now I want to thank You for Your choice of me and how You use me. Amen.*

When you think of God's choice—think of His grace and love. The result of God using you is all about God and His plan and His purpose.

God did not choose you because you were "good." No! You are "good" because God choose you. It is all about God, and He deserves the credit, praise, glory, and honor for all that He accomplishes through you.

Lord, thank You for choosing me. I don't deserve Your choice, but I am grateful for Your choice of me. So I will try to walk worthy of Your calling, and I will give praise to You for Your grace. Amen.

Read: Ephesians 1:3-14

Day 04

Past and Future

May the God before whom my grandfather Abraham and my father, Isaac, walked…bless these boys…may their descendants multiply greatly throughout the earth

(Genesis 48:15–16, NLT).

When Jacob was blessing his grandsons, he identified them with God's past history of working in the family. The boys had probably heard the stories about great-grandfather Abraham. Now Jacob's blessing tied them to that historical heritage. That would be a formable foundation on which the boys could build their lives. Just as God had intervened in the past to give victory to their fathers and grandfathers, so now the boys were reminded God would do it for them. Jacob's reminding them of the past would build faith into the two boys who would be leaders in the future.

Lord, help me remember my spiritual parents and how they helped frame my future. Help me learn from examples of Abraham, Isaac, and Jacob. Then help me pass these lessons on to future generations. Amen.

But Jacob was doing more than building on the past. He directed their faith to the future: "multiply your descendants." And isn't true biblical faith grounded on two truths? The past, what God has done, and the future, what God can do and will do. To be successful in your Christian life, make sure of your past anchor of salvation and then your future anchors of what God will do for you.

Lord, strengthen my faith in Your past work in my salvation and leading in my life. Then give me future faith in what You will do in my life. I yield my past and future to You. Amen.

Read: Genesis 25:16-34

DAY 05

CHEATING

No wonder his name is Jacob [meaning deceiver], *for now he has cheated me twice. First he took my rights as the firstborn, and now he has stolen my blessing*

(Genesis 27:36, NLT).

There is an old saying, "Cheat me once—your problem. Cheat me twice—my problem." In today's reading the older son Esau announced for all to hear that his younger brother Jacob tricked him out of his firstborn privilege. That is when Jacob swindled hungry brother Esau out of his birth privilege for a bowl of stew. It was the tempting aroma of cooking meat that weakened older brother Esau to bargain away his lifelong "right" to satisfy a hunger pain in his body. While Jacob had the "long-range" vision of the future, Esau had short-range hunger pangs.

Lord, help me learn value from the two brothers. Help me value the future and be willing to sacrifice immediate pleasure for the long-range values in life. Keep me from making "snap" decisions— that are wrong decisions—just because of the immediate pleasure of the moment. Amen.

There was a second time Jacob plotted to gain future benefits. It was when Jacob deceived his father Isaac—who was blind—by cooking meat from the "home herd" and then dressed like Esau to deceive his father. We condemn Jacob for lying and deceiving his father, but at the same time commend him for desiring the inheritance and the positive spiritual benefits that go with the inheritance.

> *Lord, I will always tell the truth, because I see Jesus who is the Truth. I will not mispresent myself to others, because that is a strategy of satan. I will serve You as honestly as I can. Amen.*

Read: Genesis 27:1-46

DAY 06

BIBLICAL ADOPTION

Now I am claiming as my own sons these two boys of yours, Ephraim and Manasseh

(Genesis 48:5, NLT).

According to scholars, this action by Jacob was the "legal" adoption of these two grandsons. Think about the situation. The two boys were born to an Egyptian woman and Joseph. If any would question the biblical basis of these two boys to be spiritual leaders among the 12 tribes of Israel, Jacob answered any criticism. These two boys would be the heads of two prominent tribes/states among God's people. They would also have a growing influence among God's people/nation. Because of the future importance of this event, who can deny God gave prophetic revelation to old Jacob?

> *Lord, You know the hearts of all—young and old alike. You knew what these two boys would do when You led old Jacob to include them in the prophetic blessing of his grandsons who would lead the future tribes of Israel. Amen.*

But Jacob did more than direct the future affairs of Israel. Jacob brought God into the equation when he began, *"God Almighty appeared to me"* (Genesis 48:3). Jacob wanted all to know that God was not only the source of the blessing on Israel, God was also the One who directed and guided his life and the lives of all the family. By bringing God into the conversation, Jacob directed everyone's thinking to the blessing on His people.

> *Lord, thank You for choosing Jacob and using him. You used Jacob even though he was a "trickster." That means You can use me. I confess my sins, forgive me. I plead for Your guidance, lead me. Amen.*

Read: Genesis 48:1-22

DAY 07

DO RIGHT

God Almighty appeared to me at Luz in the land of Canaan and blessed me

(Genesis 48:3, NLT).

Jacob was old and his health was failing. When his younger son Joseph came to visit, the elder did not talk about all the events and successes of his life. Since the old man did not have much time left, he focused on God's intervention in his life and how his encounter with the Lord changed everything. When you don't have much time, place your priority on the important. Jacob told how his life was changed/transformed with God showing up; that gave him focus. Learn the lesson of making the main thing in life the main thing.

Lord, teach me the lesson of priority. Help me follow the rules set by Paul, "For me, to live is Christ" (Philippians 1:21). Forgive me when I have let my selfish agenda rule my schedule. Help me learn that I'll never get a second opportunity to make a good first decision. Amen.

Jacob made many mistakes, and we can learn from his life to not make the same types of mistakes. We can also turn from Jacob's negative lessons to see the good/positive things he did in life. We can learn both negative and positive lessons from his life. It will be to our benefit.

Lord, I only get one life to live for You. Help me learn from the good examples of others to always do right. Also, remind me of my positive and negative experiences to always do right. Help me think right, plan right, and do right. Amen.

Read: Genesis 48:1-22

DAY 08

LEARNING HOW TO CHOOSE RIGHT

The man's name was Elimelech, and his wife was Naomi. Their two sons were Mahlon and Chilion. They were Ephrathites from Bethlehem in the land of Judah. They left and went to the land of Moab, they settled there. Then Elimelech died, and Naomi was left with her two sons

(Ruth 1:2-3, ELT).

Naomi and Elimelech were identified as Ephrathites living in Bethlehem. This phrase suggested they were "upper class" and "financially successful." Since they were among the best, they expected the best. When famine hit Bethlehem, which means "house of bread," and there was little to no bread, they left to go to Moab. From places in Bethlehem they could actually see and were attracted to the well-watered plains of Moab. They allowed physical conditions to determine their spiritual destiny. What they thought would be a land of plenty turned out to be a land of death. Elimelech and the two sons died. This left Naomi with two daughters-in-law. To the credit of Naomi, she made the correct decision when it seemed everything turned against her. She decided to return to her home, her people, and her God.

Lord, help me learn from Naomi how to make good/better decisions. Give me "spiritual eyes" to see beyond the good/alterative things in life. Help me see Your will/plan for Your people and give me courage in always choosing right. Amen.

If every decision Naomi made was "wrong," let's give her credit for at least finally making the right decision. While Naomi's advice to her two daughters-in-law was wrong, at least she choose right. What does that tell us about life? It is never too late to make the right decision. She choose God, His country, His people. She choose right.

Lord, help me learn how to make good decisions, then give me courage to follow and do what is right. Then remind me of the bad decisions I have made and my selfish basis for my poor decisions. Help me to think right, plan right, choose right, do right, and give You credit. Amen.

Read: Ruth 1:1-22

Day 09

Empty

I went away full, but the Lord has brought me home empty
(Ruth 1:21, NLT).

Naomi finally gave a correct assessment of her life when she arrived back in Bethlehem. She realized what she had when she left Bethlehem. Honesty is the first step to self-correction. But she went a step further with her honesty. She admitted failure when she testified to coming back *empty*. Sometimes a person must realize how empty they are before God will return to fill their life. Since Jesus is the *Truth* (John 14:6), He will honor those who come to Him truthfully. What matter/attitude must you confess to God to become truthful before Him?

> *Lord, I confess my spiritual blindness when I did not see Your work in my life. Forgive me for unrepented sin and obstinance to Your plan for my life. Cleanse me with the blood of Jesus (1 John 1:7-10). Amen.*

One of the best places to be in life is *empty*. Naomi confessed she was empty, but also in her confession she admitted her sin and the decisions that made her empty. When you know your gas tank is empty, it's a good time to fill it up. When you confess to God you are empty, it's time to fill up!

Lord, I am empty and it scares me. I am empty and I want to be filled with Your Person. I am empty and I want Your power to keep me going for You. I am empty and I cannot do anything to serve You in ministry. Come Holy Spirit, fill me. I am waiting. Amen.

Read: Romans 3:1-31

DAY 10

THINK POSITIVE

Things are far more bitter for me than for you, because the Lord himself has raised his fist against me

(Ruth 1:13, NLT).

Naomi blamed God for everything that had gone against her. Do you know anyone who blames God for the *bad* things in life? Have you done that? Notice she used the picture of a *fist*. Isn't a fist a part of your body to express anger? She wasn't saying God defeated her with His divine fist. No! When you blame God for all the problems in your life, you are probably backsliding like Naomi. She left God's land of promise; left the Temple, God's dwelling place; left God's people; and left her heritage. Backsliding people don't see God's goodness; they usually blame God for all their troubles.

Lord, keep me from backsliding; keep me from blaming You for problems; keep me from bitterness. Forgive me for past times when I complained, help me see Your work in my life, and help me praise You for who You are. Amen.

Are you a *bitter* person? Or are you an *optimistic* person? What is usually the difference? God! When you are *spiritually right* with God and problems come, you usually have faith and ask God to help you get through them. When good times come, again you see God's hand and praise Him. What must you do with any *bitterness* you find in your heart?

Lord, thank You for hearing me in my good days and in my bad days. Thank You for Your mercy and forgiveness. Today I come just as I am. Forgive me, redirect me, fill me, use me. I thank You ahead of time for Your grace. Amen.

Read: John 7:37-39; Acts 2:41-47

DAY 11

GOD'S PLAN

She [Ruth] found herself working in a field that belonged to Boaz, the relative of her father-in-law, Elimelech

(Ruth 2:3, NLT).

Circumstances are a part of life and yet become the fabric that makes up your life. Did your father and mother just happen to meet each other? Yet you are the outcome of that happenstance. When Ruth went looking for a field in which to glean (pick grain), it happened to belong to a distant relative of the family. God knows all things—past, present, and future—because He is the eternal, omnipresent God who lives in the future. God was working His plan (Jeremiah 29:11) for Naomi and Ruth. But also God was working His plan that would lead to the birth of Jesus Christ (Matthew 1:5).

Lord, teach me to look for Your hand in the small details of life. Thank You for my parents and thank You for my education thus far. Help me to trust You—and follow You—as You continue to work/lead in my life. Amen.

God saw the deep, life-changing decision Ruth made to become a part of the family. Also, God saw her character and used her to be the great-grandmother of David. While the details of the book of Ruth seem small and insignificant, nothing is small or insignificant to God. He uses small and great events to work His plans on earth. In the same way, God uses people—both famous and unknown—to accomplish His purpose. What is God doing in your life?

Lord, open my "spiritual eyes" to see what You are doing in my life. Then give me courage to do what You are leading me to do and help me become what You are molding me to become. Amen.

Read: Ruth 2:1-23

DAY 12

BOAZ

While she was there, Boaz arrived from Bethlehem and greeted the harvesters. "The Lord be with you!" he said. "The Lord bless you!" the harvesters replied

(Ruth 2:4, NLT).

Boaz was a good man. Even before we see him doing good deeds, Boaz had a habit of being good. He greeted his workers pointing them to God, "The Lord be with you." Most employers do not have an outward expression of faith in God. Boaz had a daily relationship with God, as evident in the way he greeted his employees. As you read the story, we see a healthy attitude between boss and workers. Whenever you get into management, let Boaz's attitude influence you.

Lord, thank You for the example of Boaz's respect for You and for his workers. Give me that attitude in life and help me be an example of Your grace to all I work for, work with, and those I supervise. Amen.

Note that Boaz was not reluctant to use God's name when he greeted his workers: "the Lord be with you." He used God's name, *Lord*, which is used by God's people; he did not use the other title, *God*, which is used primarily by the unsaved. Look again at the story—all Boaz did and said reflected his high regard for the Lord and for the way He wanted His people to do business.

Lord, I come bowing before Your name, Jehovah—Lord. You are the "I AM" of Heaven. You are the Almighty Lord, and I worship You and praise You for all You are and have done. Amen.

Read: Ruth 3:1-18

DAY 13

THE LAW AND TRADITION

And with the land I have acquired Ruth, the Moabite widow of Mahlon, to be my wife. This way she can have a son to carry on the family name of her dead husband and to inherit the family property here in his hometown. You are all witnesses today

(Ruth 4:10, NLT).

Boaz wanted to do everything according to law and tradition. So he went to the city gate and called to the owner of the "bankruptcy note" on Elimelech's property. They negotiated the selling price of the property so that Boaz not only owned the property—because he was close kin—but he gained the right to marry Ruth. God was working through the laws and traditions of that day to legally allow Boaz to marry Ruth. Of course, in the process, Ruth became great-grandmother to King David.

Lord, just as Your people worked through the laws of their land, help me to work through the laws where I live so I can serve You better. Amen.

Law, whether written or understood, is the basis for civilization. Law gives to each the rights of property, life, liberty, and the pursuit of happiness. And what is law? It is an extension of God. For God is law, and law is the extension of His power and control over the universe and humans living on earth. In other words, law is one of God's attributes.

Lord, forgive me when I have fought Your laws—either spiritual law, human law, or legal law. Help me understand Your nature and how You use law to control, guide, and accomplish Your purpose on earth and among people. Amen.

Read: Ruth 4:1-22

Day 14

Spiritual Children

There is a son born to Naomi

(Ruth 4:17).

Ruth and Boaz gave birth to a son—Obed. It is interesting that the Bible describes the boy being born to Naomi. Obviously Ruth was the mother, but remember she was from Moab. The son is identified with his grandmother because Obed would carry on the family line/tradition in Israel. Another thing, Ruth would have been busy taking care of the household duties for Boaz, looking after the household budget and supplies, as well as management of the servants. So Naomi took over duties of child-raising. Maybe Naomi was better qualified to teach young Obed Jewish traditions/practices, because Ruth was not raised according to Jewish traditions. Sometimes *practical* wins out in the struggle against tradition.

> *Lord, thank You for Ruth, a Gentile—a Moabite—who is included in the genealogy of Jesus Christ. I am also a Gentile and partaker in the benefits of Jesus Christ. Thank You for Ruth's salvation and for mine. Amen.*

One more thing about Naomi being identified with Obed. The child became famous because he was identified with King David. For that to be meaningful, Obed was identified in the line through Naomi—the Jewish line.

Lord, I praise You for the faithfulness of Naomi. She made a difficult decision to return to Your people, the Jews, and to Your holy land. May I learn faithfulness in difficult situations, just as she was faithful in a difficult situation. Thank You for honoring her by identifying her with Obed, her grandson. I don't seek glory or honor for myself, but may I lead people to faith in Christ; may I have spiritual children and grandchildren. Amen.

Read: Ruth 3:1-18

DAY 15

THE LORD, THE GOD OF ELIJAH

He struck the water with Elijah's cloak and cried out, "Where is the Lord, the God of Elijah?" Then the river divided, and Elisha went across

(2 Kings 2:14, ELT).

What did young Elisha want? He wanted more than the old prophet's cloak. The young prophet wanted the Lord God in his life and in his ministry. He cried out, "Where is the Lord, the God of Elijah?" What else would matter to the young prophet if he didn't get the presence of God in his life? Yes, the young prophet got the "prophet's cloak," but even when he used it to divide the waters of Jordan, the power was not in clothing—it was in God. Let's be careful in ministry that we don't imitate others' actions, phrases, or even their attitude. Let's make sure we get "the Lord, the God of Elijah."

Lord, I pray for the spirit of Elijah to be in my life. But I am not comparing myself to him or envying the things Elijah had. No! I want You, the Lord, the God of Elijah to anoint me for ministry and use me to serve You. Amen.

When young Elisha got ready to do his first miracle, he was wise enough to ask for the power that Elijah had—he asked for "the Lord, the God of Elijah." God is honored when we call on Him to do what He can do and what He wants to do. When we honor God, He answers our requests.

Lord, I ask for You, the Lord, the God of Elijah, to bless me and use me. Give me strong faith to trust You for Your power in my ministry, and I want Your influence working in the lives of those to whom I minister. Amen.

Read: 1 Kings 17:1-24

DAY 16

SEAL OF APPROVAL

And as the chariot and Elijah disappeared from sight, Elisha tore his clothes in distress. Elisha picked up Elijah's cloak which had fallen
(2 Kings 2:12-13, ELT).

If young Elisha wanted to carry on the official ministry of old Elijah, he got a pictorial transfer of the office. The prophet's cloak was symbolic of his office, and it told those watching who was now in that position/office. So young Elisha not only was given the challenge/office of old Elijah, he got the symbol of the office—the cloak. But having a man's coat was nothing if he did not have the man's authority/spiritual power. Immediately the young man used the cloak to strike and part the Jordan River. The power in ministry was everything—not the symbolic coat. In your life, don't seek another's office, title, or act like them. Make God your power, your authority, and your office. Let them see God's power in your life.

Lord, I don't want to just be like other believers and act like them. Lord, I want Your presence in my life/ministry. I want Your "seal of approval" on all I am and do. May others see Your presence in my life as they feel Your power in my ministry. Amen.

When old Elijah left, what did young Elisha get? He got the old prophet's cloak, but much more—young Elisha got the old man's blessing and approval. He got the old man's office and he served the Lord. He got the old man's power that did seven miracles, but the young prophet did fourteen miracles. He did get a double portion.

Lord, I don't want to be like others, and I don't want just a double portion of Your presence. I want more—I want as much power as You can give me. I want as much of Your presence as You can give. Amen.

Read: 1 Kings 18:1-19

Day 17

Asking for a Hard Thing

You have asked a hard thing

(2 Kings 2:10).

Was this a hard thing for God to answer? No! No miracle is too hard for God. Did old Elijah think this was going to be a hard lesson for him to teach the young prophet? Probably not! Perhaps the old prophet was thinking this was going to be hard for young Elisha to learn. The old prophet knew some of the hard lessons he had learned. It was hard living in the wilderness being fed by ravens for several years. It was hard to live with a widow in Zarephath, and God did supply oil and grain daily for them to eat. Old Elijah knew about his difficulties, and he wanted to challenge the young prophet to be ready for hard times in the future.

Lord, I have had hard times in the past, and You have provided. Thank You for the lessons I have learned. There are difficulties today; thank You for the lessons You are teaching me. There will be problems and hard times in the future—prepare me for these. Amen.

No parent wants their child to go through hard times, because parents love their children and they want to make it as easy as possible for them. Yet life-changing lessons are learned in difficult situations. Life-changing lessons are learned with practice, discipline, and self-sacrifice. We must bring that same attitude into our spiritual growth. Hard lessons make disciples who are hardened against sin and disciples who will not give up. No, hard lessons are the foundation for a life ready to live for God and serve Him.

Lord, prepare me for hard lessons. When I complain, remind me I have asked for difficult things. When I think of quitting, give me courage to go forward. Give me kind lessons to make my faith solid as a rock. Amen.

Read: 1 Kings 18:20-46

DAY 18

A DOUBLE PORTION

Please let a double portion of your spirit be upon me

(2 Kings 2:9).

Do you always know what you should ask for from God when you pray? Probably not! Sometimes we just go to prayer to worship or praise or meditate on the Lord. The young prophet Elisha knew what to ask for—a double portion of Elijah's spirit. What a magnificent request. Would you ask God for a double portion of the spirit that was on the person who led or preached when you were converted? That is a valid prayer that will lead to your growth spiritually—more faith, more ministry, more usefulness in His service. Why don't you make it your prayer request this week?

> *Lord, I want a double portion of Your Spirit that was on the one who was responsible for my salvation. Help me influence someone to salvation just as I was influenced to become a Christian. And, Lord, let me influence someone to be saved—many! Amen.*

Old Elijah had said to young Elisha, "*If you see me when I am taken from you, then you will get your request*" (2 Kings 2:10, NLT). Because if you ask for a double portion of God's Spirit, there are things you must do to receive an answer to your request. You may have to study, witness to someone, make sacrifices, etc. If you want God to work in your life, you must be willing to work for Him.

Lord, I want a double portion of Your Spirit, and I will double up on my ministry for You. I will do more than I am doing now for You. Give me courage and strength and determination and spiritual power. Amen.

Read: 1 Kings 19:1-21

DAY 19

WATCHING FROM A DISTANCE

Fifty men from the group of prophets also went and watched from a distance as Elijah and Elisha stopped beside the Jordan River
(2 Kings 2:7, NLT).

Did you notice that two of God's servants were involved in walking and heading to meet God? Also, there were 50 sons of the prophets watching from a distance. Some people are involved in God's work and they walk daily with God. But others just watch God work from a distance. How did the 50 learn of Elijah's departure but not get involved? If you had been there that day, would you have wanted to walk with Elijah as he was heading to meet the Lord? There will always be "watchers" in God's work, and there will always be those walking with God and being faithful to God. Make a commitment to always walk with God and serve God (Colossians 2:6).

Lord, give me wisdom to do the right thing at church or with other believers. Give me wisdom when to "walk and pray," and make me a person of action when I should get involved, minister, and be faithful. Amen.

The 50 sons of the prophets did not walk with Elijah and Elisha. Maybe they were just observers, but at least they were present to see the action and to talk to Elijah. Let's not be too quick to criticize them. Maybe they were doing what was expected of them. As for you—sometimes you serve at church, sometimes you worship. At least you are there when God shows up, just like He sent the chariot of fire for Elijah.

Lord, I will "show up" when You call me to service. I will work when You challenge me with ministry. I will pray when You put a burden on my heart. I will be faithful. Amen.

Read: 1 Kings 21:1-24

DAY 20

DEPARTURE DAY

When the Lord was about to take Elijah up to heaven in a whirlwind,
Elijah and Elisha were traveling from Gilgal
(2 Kings 2:1, NLT).

How would you plan if you knew you were going to meet God this day? We don't know how Elijah found out it was "departure day." But others knew it was going to happen. "*And the sons of the prophets that were at Jericho came to Elisha, and said unto him, Knowest thou that the Lord will take away thy master from thy head to day?*" (2 Kings 2:5, KJV). Elijah did not let others "shake him up." Elijah just kept walking from Bethel down the mountain across the Jordan River, until he was carried to Heaven. Would you plan your activities the same as Elijah if you knew God was taking you to Heaven this day?

Lord, help me live in Your presence day by day and second by second. Thank You for Jesus indwelling my heart. If I die, I will go with Jesus to meet my heavenly Father. Give me the faith of Elijah to just keep walking and doing what I have to do. Amen.

There were several who talked to Elijah about the developing crisis. But his answer was the same, "*Yea, I know it; hold ye your peace*" (2 Kings 2:5, KJV). Do you have that deep inner assurance you are a child of God? Are you as ready to meet God face to face as Elijah was prepared? Can you face the prospect of dying with confidence? Elijah had that confidence, and you are just as important to God as was Elijah.

> *Lord, I am ready to meet You face to face. Forgive all my sins and failures—even the times I displeased You. And forgive those times I forgot about You. But thank You for remembering because You know all things, all the time. Amen.*

Read: 2 Kings 2:1-18

DAY 21

WHAT ARE YOUR NEEDS?

For this is what the Lord, the God of Israel, says: There will always be flour and olive oil left in your containers until the time when the Lord sends rain and the crops grow again!

(1 Kings 17:14)

Elijah finished his ministry just as he began—fully trusting God. When we first read of Elijah, he was fed twice daily by ravens. Then we read how God supernaturally supplied flour and oil at the widow's home in Zarephath. Just as God provided for the needs of Elijah, you should trust God to supply your needs in all areas of your life. *"My God shall supply all your need according to His riches in glory by Christ Jesus"* (Philippians 4:19). God may not supply all you want, but look again at the promise. He will supply *needs*. What is your need today—spiritual, physical, financial, mental, or perhaps you have a particular need.

Lord, I look to You to provide for my needs. Sometimes I need a job with pay; sometimes I need physical strength; sometimes my need is unique to me. Give me faith to trust You and give me boldness to pray for answers. Amen.

God provided for Elijah in a way that was not customary or usual. God used ravens, which are scavenger birds, and he used a poor widow without a job or husband. God may provide for you in an unusual way. Also remember God supplies our needs—not our desires or dreams or wishes.

When you live out your "need" level, you are in a place where God can provide.

Lord, teach me how to pray for my needs and give me faith to trust Your provision. Forgive me when I trust my "want" list because it is sometimes loaded with my "wish" list. Amen.

Read: I Kings 17:1-24

DAY 22

BECOME A DISCIPLE-MAKER

Two disciples followed Jesus. Andrew first found his own brother and pointed him to Jesus. John also found his brother. "We have found the Messiah, the Christ"

(John 1:35-42, ELT).

John was probably 17 years old when he began following Jesus as a disciple. He joined his youthful friend Andrew to go learn more about Jesus. They had been disciples of John the Baptist, which suggests they were spiritually alert, looking for the Messiah. When both men talked with Jesus, they wanted to bring their brothers to be Jesus' disciples. The greatest thing about John's integrity was he did what Jesus said regarding the Great Commission: *"Go be disciple-makers"* (Matthew 28:18, ELT). John's older brother James followed Jesus; so did Andrew's older brother Peter. If you are going to be a true follower of Jesus, ask God to make you a disciple-maker.

> *Jesus, give me a burden to find someone to be Your disciple. Help me approach them and help me lead them to follow You. Not just one person, make me a lifelong disciple-maker. Give me wisdom, compassion, persuasive ability, and teaching ability. Amen.*

It is significant that John got his older brother James to follow Jesus. Both boys had worked as fishermen with their father Zebedee, a successful fisherman. The father had more than one fishing boat; he used the boys and hired help (Mark 1:20). It was a sacrifice to leave their father and the business to follow Jesus, but both boys did so. When they turned their back on their father's business, they gave up future financial prosperity to follow Jesus. What have you given up?

Lord, thank You for the example of John giving up all to follow You. I too give You everything. I will follow You, serve You, and minister for You. Use me to change the lives of others as You have changed my life. Amen.

Read: Mark 1:11-20; Luke 5:1-11

DAY 23

SONS OF THUNDER

James and John (the sons of Zebedee, but Jesus nicknamed them "Sons of Thunder")

(Mark 3:17, NLT).

Can you imagine having the nickname "sons of thunder"? It was given to them by Jesus—not friends and family. Did Jesus give them the nickname because He saw them erupt into anger, like a thunderstorm erupts? Or did Jesus use His omniscience (knowing all things, possible and actual) to nickname them? Remember, young John forbade a person for casting out demons (Mark 38:39). The youngest disciple John was enthusiastic, self-centered, and impetuous. Do you still have a youthful burst of arrogance and self-centered anger? Since Jesus transformed John into the apostle of love, what has He done for you?

> *Lord, forgive me for past anger. I will apologize to those whom I have offended. Give me love and patience that You gave to John, and help me learn to be as faithful as was John. Amen.*

What changed/transformed John? First, the Bible says he was loved by Jesus (John 13:23). When writing the gospel of John, he called himself *"the disciple whom Jesus loved"* (John 21:7). Then John is known as the apostle of love (1 John). But most of all John learned love by close identification with Jesus, leaning on Jesus' breast (John 13:23-25).

Lord, I want to be known as one who loves others. Forgive my sin of selfishness, and please give me the Spirit of Jesus. Teach me how to show love to others; take away my selfish desires and closed spiritual eyes. I want Jesus' heart of love. Come Jesus, pour Yourself into my life and let me show Your love to others. Amen.

Read: 1 John 3:1-24

DAY 24

FOLLOW JESUS

A little farther Jesus saw James and John in a boat repairing their nets. "Follow Me"

(Mark 1:19-20, ELT).

And Peter looking back saw John, "What shall this man do?" Jesus answered, "If I want him to remain alive until I return what is that to you? Follow Me"

(John 21:21-22, ELT).

At the beginning of Jesus' ministry He called John to follow Him. Then in His post-resurrection appearance, again Jesus commanded all, "Follow Me." What a great way to begin and end your life. When you first were saved, you began following Jesus. Therefore, follow Jesus right up to the end of your life. As Jesus called His disciples, for most of them, their call was "Follow Me." How clear, how concise, how simple. It is not about what you want to do; it is about following Jesus. It is not about how smart, how attractive, how popular—it is, "Follow Me." Are you following Jesus? Have you talked to Him today? Have you talked to others about Him?

Lord, I said I would follow You when I was saved. Forgive any stumbles. Thank You for Your presence in my life, and thank You for Your direction. May I serve You, please You, and win someone to follow You, just as I have followed You. Amen.

Jesus said, "Follow Me," when He first met John. Then Jesus said it again right before He returned to Heaven. So Jesus meant for us to follow Him. This is more important than joining a church. Following Jesus is more important than Christian activities. Following Jesus is the foundation of what you believe, how you live, and will be your hope when you die. When you follow Jesus, you are with Him, and He is indwelling you.

Lord Jesus, I will follow You in obedience to Your call. I will follow You because it is Your desire. I will follow You because I get to be with You. Amen.

Read: Mark 1:16-20; John 21:18-25

DAY 25

EXPECTATION DAY

Now there stood by the cross of Jesus His mother…When Jesus there-
fore saw His mother, and the disciple whom He loved standing by, He
said to His mother, "Woman, behold your son!" Then He said to the
disciple, "Behold your mother!" And from that hour that disciple took
her to his own home

(John 19:25-27).

Who do you ask to help when the task is not only important, it's imper-
ative? You ask someone you trust, but not everyone you trust can do what
you have asked. So when it is imperative, you ask a trusted friend who is most
likely to help you and has the ability and resources to do it. On the cross
Jesus asked John to take care of His mother. Note—John was trustworthy;
Jesus had trusted the youngest disciple previously on important missions.
But John owned a home in Jerusalem, so Mary could live in that house.
John's father Zebedee apparently had a prosperous business, but Zebedee
was dead at this time. So John had the resources to take care of Mary.

Lord, You asked John because he was trustworthy. I want to serve
You and I want to be trustworthy. Forgive my sins and weaknesses
and help me be strong and trustworthy. Teach me what I need to
learn and lead me what to do to become more trustworthy. Amen.

But there is another reason why Jesus choose John. John was the apostle of love, and Jesus wanted a loving person to care for His mother. Not

all people who would be physically and financially able to care for Mary would be as kind to her as John. When Jesus committed Mary to John's care, our Lord was fulfilling His responsibility as the oldest son in the family. Jesus *finished well.*

Lord, thank You for the example of Jesus' care for His mother. Give me compassion to care for my family as best as I can, as long as I can. May I follow the example of Jesus who fulfilled the fifth commandment, "Honor your father and your mother" (Exodus 20:12). Amen.

Read: John 20:1-30

DAY 26

JOHN WAS FAITHFUL

Peter and John went to the tomb early Sunday morning. Both ran, but younger John outran him. John reached the tomb first and looked in but did not enter. Peter ran straight in, and they saw the linen cloth wrapped together

(John 20:4-7, ELT).

Ten disciples fled into the night when Jesus was arrested. The eleventh, Judas, hanged himself, but John was faithful to follow Jesus. He came to Caiaphas' house where Jesus was tried (John 18:16). He followed Jesus to the cross—and brought Mary, Jesus' mother (John 19:21). He was first at the tomb on Easter Sunday morning (John 20:2-3) and was the first to recognize the resurrected Jesus on the shore of Lake Galilee (John 21:7). You could describe John as a "faithful disciple." He was always there when needed. Are you a faithful follower of Jesus? Do you always show up at church? Prayer meetings? Where are you supposed to be?

Lord, thank You for the example of John and his faithfulness. Help me follow the Lord as John followed Jesus. Help me be faithful to my responsibilities to You. I want to serve You, extend Your ministry, and glorify Your name. Make me faithful. Amen.

When the church was persecuted and Christians scattered everywhere, John and the disciples stayed in Jerusalem (Acts 8:1). When Paul first got saved and visited Jerusalem, he met John and the other church leaders

(Galatians 2:9). What can be said of John is he was faithful! Can that be said of you?

Lord, I want to be faithful in all I say and do and the things I am known for. Forgive my weaknesses, failings, and sins. Use me to encourage others and motivate them to serve You. Help me follow the example of John and be always faithful. Amen.

Read: Mark 14:3; John 19:26; 20:2-3; 21:1-7; Acts 8:1; Galatians 2:7

DAY 27

SEEING JESUS IN HEAVEN

I heard behind me a loud voice…I turned to see…One like the Son of Man…. "Do not be afraid; I Am the First and the Last"
(Revelation 1:10, 12-13, 17).

Because John was faithful in life to follow Jesus, he was given the privilege as an elderly man (age 90) to see Jesus in an apocalyptical vision. He saw the glorified Jesus in Heaven, and he recognized Him as the physical Jesus he followed in Galilee. John lived longer than the other disciples. Why? Perhaps because they ran away the night Jesus was arrested, but John did not. They were martyred, but John lived to approximately 100 years of age and died peacefully. Because John followed Jesus and faced death, he was permitted to see the living Jesus in Heaven. Now you can see Jesus through John's eyes as you read the Book of Revelation.

Lord, thank You for the faithfulness of John. Help me learn from him and help me be as faithful as John. He died a natural death. I don't know if I will die naturally or if I will be a martyr, but I know I will see You in Heaven. Amen.

When you look through John's eyes to see Jesus in the Book of Revelation, you see a glorified Jesus. He will be like that when you and I get to Heaven. Read from John's words so you will recognize Jesus when you get to Heaven.

Lord, I look forward to being with You in Heaven. I don't look forward to dying; none of us do. Give me strength to live for You, and give me courage to die well and come to live with You in Heaven. Thank You that John showed me the way. Amen.

Read: Revelation 1:1-20

DAY 28

SEEING THE FUTURE

Then I saw heaven opened, and a white horse was standing there. Its rider was named Faithful and True, for he judges fairly and wages a righteous war. His eyes were like flames of fire, and on his head were many crowns. A name was written on him that no one understood except himself

(Revelation 19:11-12, NLT).

John was given the privilege of seeing the future—he saw Jesus on a white horse standing in Heaven. Jesus was preparing to return to the earth to make war with the antichrist and all the evil ones following him. Jesus has always held out His arms inviting people to come to Him for salvation (Matthew 11:28-30). But the people on earth have rejected God the Father and His salvation. They have the mark of the antichrist—666—and they are resolved in their hatred to God and His righteousness. Jesus is coming to make war with them to cast them into hell. This is a horrible picture that John writes for us, but it is the truth, and it must be said.

Lord, thank You for saving me, and thank You for giving me a new nature so I can know Your righteousness and judgment. I do not like the picture of the many who rebel against You and will be judged. I will try to witness to as many of my family and friends as possible. Use me as a testimony to them. Amen.

111

When Jesus returns to earth, there will be no second chance to get saved. Those who are judged have hated God and will continue to hate Him to the end. God loves them, and Jesus died for them. But our God of love is also a God who must act according to truth and judge them for their sins. The Book of Revelation has difficult pictures, but God doesn't turn His back on difficulties. Jesus suffered and died for our sins, and now He must come to judge those who have refused Him.

Jesus, You are love—thank You for loving me and dying for me. I pray for all my family and friends who are not saved. Help me speak to them about Jesus and His wonderful salvation. Save them. Thank You for my salvation. Amen.

Read: Revelation 19:1-21

DAY 29

PAUL DID NOT START WELL

I was circumcised when I was eight days old. I am a pure-blooded citizen of Israel and a member of the tribe of Benjamin—a real Hebrew if there ever was one! I was a member of the Pharisees, who demand the strictest obedience to the Jewish law. I was so zealous that I harshly persecuted the church. And as for righteousness, I obeyed the law without fault
(Philippians 3:5-6, NLT).

At that time a great persecution arose against the church which was at Jerusalem; and they were all scattered throughout the regions of Judea and Samaria, except the apostles…As for Saul, he made havoc of the church, entering every house, and dragging off men and women, committing them to prison
(Acts 8:1-3).

Paul started out in the wrong direction, doing the wrong things, for the wrong motivation. He tried to wipe out the existence of the church; he was even ready to kill people who disagreed with him. But Paul met Jesus Christ on the road to Damascus and was radically changed when he was supernaturally transformed by God's grace. That means if you started out wrong—like Paul—you can be radically transformed by Jesus Christ. The "Christ" he fought came into Paul's life to transform him—because that is what Jesus does. He began with 100 percent of his energy persecuting the church, and he ended up giving 100 percent of his energy and life to expand the church.

Lord, thank You for the miracle in Paul's life. I ask for a miracle in my life. I want to give 100 percent of my energy to proclaim the message of Jesus Christ to the world. Forgive me for any hesitancy to serve You or any negative thing I have said or done against You. Help me honestly proclaim the message of Jesus Christ. Amen.

What can change a radical persecutor of the church? One thing! Paul met Jesus Christ on the road to Damascus. Jesus is the One who changed Paul's life, and He can change your life. If you are stalled in your life's purpose, Jesus can get you started. If you are drifting, Jesus can push you toward a new life's goal—serving Him completely.

Lord, open my spiritual eyes to see where I am in life. Jesus, take control of my life and get me started on the walk of faith. Jesus, help me find a purpose in life may You become the focus and purpose of my life. Amen.

Read: Philippians 3:1-14

DAY 30

INDWELLING LOVE/CHRIST

I have been crucified with Christ; it is no longer I who live, but Christ lives in me; and the life which I now live in the flesh I live by faith in the Son of God, who loved me and gave Himself for me
(Galatians 2:20).

Once Paul met Jesus on the road to Damascus, it was no longer a head/mental knowledge of Jesus. Jesus became intimate to Paul; he was crucified with Him. That meant Christ died for Paul's sins, forgiving the young Paul, and giving him an intimate relationship with the Father. But also, Christ now lived in Paul, and the daily life of the apostle was directed by the faith of the Son of God. What did that mean? Powerful living! Supernatural living! Christ not only indwelt the apostle, but Christ lived His life through Paul. And with the life of Christ came the love of Christ capturing Paul and living through Paul with a purpose of preaching salvation to all the lost people in the world.

Jesus, thank You for indwelling Paul from the moment he believed in salvation. And yes, Jesus, thank You for indwelling me from the moment I was saved. May I live the victorious life that Paul lived. Use me in ministry as You used Paul. Amen.

To live the faith of the Son of God is to live supernaturally. That power is available to all who received Christ into their heart/life. He came into a life to transform it and use it. Christ lived in Paul to share His love to all, and He wants to do that for each believer He indwells. He is willing and ready to do it when they are yielded to His love and by faith, claiming His love.

> *Lord Jesus, I want Your love flowing through me to others/ the world. I yield myself to receive Your love, but more than surrendering to You, I will seek to learn Your love, experience Your love, and then share it with all. Amen.*

Read: Galatians 2:1-21

Day 31

Taking the Gospel to All

I have been following the plan spoken of in the Scriptures, where it says, "Those who have never been told about him will see, and those who have never heard of him will understand"

(Romans 15:21, NLT).

In this passage Paul lays out for you the strategy he followed in all of his ministry. He did more than preach to all; Paul wanted them to clearly see the gospel. Also, he wanted all people who heard him to understand Jesus died for them to take away their sins, and the Savior arose from the grave to give them life—resurrected life. So who was Paul's target audience? "*Those who have never been told...those who have never heard.*" This message drove Paul to endure travel accidents (shipwrecks), difficulties (robbers), and sacrifices (sleeplessness). He did it all for Jesus who indwelt him and empowered him and motivated him.

Lord Jesus, thank You for giving Paul marching orders to take the gospel to all. I also receive those orders for my life. I will be faithful; give me strength and endurance. I want Your power flowing through me to reach the unsaved, in order for them to hear, to understand, and to be saved. Amen.

When Paul was saved he immediately received a "calling" to preach the message to the Gentiles. "*I am Jesus whom thou persecutest.... I have appeared unto thee for this purpose, to make thee a minister and a witness...*"

[to] *the Gentiles, unto whom now I send thee"* (Acts 9:5; 26:16-17). There was no doubt what Paul must do with his life. In the same way, God has a plan for your life (Jeremiah 31:17). For you to live godly, to be a godly testimony of God's grace, and to share the gospel with the lost.

Lord Jesus, thank You for using Paul to preach everywhere to all people. Use me as Your messenger; help me share the gospel with many. Amen.

Read: Romans 15:14-23; Acts 26:1-32

DAY 32

THE PRIZE

I want to know Christ and experience the mighty power that raised him from the dead. I want to suffer with him, sharing in his death... No, dear brothers and sisters, I have not achieved it, but I focus on this one thing: Forgetting the past and looking forward to what lies ahead, I press on to reach the end of the race and receive the heavenly prize for which God, through Christ Jesus, is calling us
(Philippians 3:10, 13-14, NLT).

Paul wanted to finish well both his life and ministry. He had experienced the power of Christ's resurrection and the fellowship of His suffering. Yet Paul wanted to forget all past attainments, privileges, and sufferings so he could be conformed into the image of Jesus Christ. The "high calling" of Paul's life was to live well and die well. To him that meant to live by the indwelling of Jesus Christ and preach the life-changing power of Christ. Here Paul says, "I press toward the mark of the prize." His ultimate goal was living for Christ, being used by Christ, and then dying for Christ. How close to those goals have you come in your life?

Lord, thank You for all Paul accomplished in his life. I have a desire to be all that Paul was and a desire to do all Paul accomplished. But I am weak and I fail; and at times, I have sinned away opportunities to be victorious for Jesus. Forgive me, indwell me with Your power, use me. Amen.

Paul began well at his conversion. He spent his life serving Jesus Christ and was faithful in opportunities to preach and evangelize. God tested him with several persecutions, but he was faithful to Christ. Paul always pressed toward the goal of obtaining the prize of the high calling of God.

Lord, thank You for Paul's life. May I be faithful to the task You call me to do, just as Paul was faithful in his tasks. Help me to do all You lead me to do for You. Help me to be a testimony to Your grace and forgiveness. Use me in service and ministry. Amen.

Read: Philippians 3:1-21

DAY 33

TO FINISH WELL

The time of my death is near

(2 Timothy 4:6, NLT).

Finishing well—that is a theme learned by Paul. He was ready to die and had just about accomplished all God intended for him to accomplish. Note the victory cry, "I have fought the good fight." Paul's life was never easy, but he fought evil and served Jesus Christ to the end. Paul said he had "finished the race." Yes, our ministry is a race in which we train and discipline to do our best. We run against others but our eyes are on the goal. Paul finished the race well. Now there is a prize awaiting for him at the finish line. Have you raced well? Have you kept your eye on the finish line? Do you know there is a prize waiting for you?

Lord, thank You for the example of Paul. I want to "run well" as Paul ran. Give me strength and forgive me for not being stronger to race better. I want to "finish well" as Paul finished. Amen.

Paul was aware that he had not yet achieved the ultimate prize in life. This was out in front of him, motivating him to continue serving the Lord till he crossed the finish line. Paul's aim was to finish well—the theme of this book. Paul said he joined, *"all who eagerly look forward to his appearing"* (2 Timothy 4:8, NLT).

Lord, I will give You my best; forgive my past errors. I am not in the best shape to run. Give me strength to run, give me courage not to give up. Help me finish well. Amen.

Read: 2 Timothy 4:1-22

DAY 34

DYING DAILY

I face death daily

(1 Corinthians 15:31, NLT).

When did Paul die? First, he died with Christ the moment he was saved (Galatians 2:20). This means when Jesus was nailed to the cross to die for the sins of the world, the sins of Paul were also nailed to the cross. He died vicariously then. Then daily Paul surrendered his life to Christ and the sins he committed that day were forgiven experientially, so he died daily. But there is another aspect of dying daily. There were agents of satan who would murder the soul if they could. So in that sense, Paul faced the possibility of death daily. When did you die? Did you die vicariously with Christ when you were saved? Have you faced death today?

Lord, thank You for the human example of Paul who faced death to serve You. I will follow the example of Paul. I will serve You as I am willing to die daily for Jesus Christ. Use me, guide me, protect me. Amen.

Today's reading tells of the death Paul faced daily. It could mean Paul surrendered his life to Christ each day and died daily. It also could mean Paul faced death each day, meaning actual physical death. Because of what it means, we should put our life in God's hands and commit our life to God each day.

Lord, I am ready to die physically for You. Also I want to die in identification with Christ. Both ways, I want Christ to dwell in me in this life and to be glorified in my death. Amen.

Read: 1 Corinthians 15:1-32

DAY 35

THANK YOU, LORD JESUS

In everything we do, we show that we are true ministers of God. We patiently endure troubles and hardships and calamities of every kind. We have been beaten, been put in prison, faced angry mobs, worked to exhaustion, endured sleepless nights, and gone without food. …We faithfully preach the truth. God's power is working in us. We use the weapons of righteousness in the right hand for attack and the left hand for defense

(2 Corinthians 6:4-5, 7, NLT).

Paul had the greatest privilege of seeing Christ when he was saved, when Christ spoke to him in a vision (2 Corinthians 12:1-4). Paul was used by Christ to preach and open doors of evangelism to reach the multitudes. His reward in Heaven will be well earned, but think about the liabilities of serving Christ. In today's reading he mentions hardships, beatings, imprisonment, exhaustion, going without food, etc. There will be rewards for those negative experiences as well as the positive accomplishments. Compare your life to Paul—what have you accomplished for God? Also, what physical punishment have you endured? Whether easy or hard, we do it all for Christ.

Lord Jesus, thank You for all the punishment You suffered for me. Any hardships I face will be nothing compared to Your sufferings. Thank You for the privilege of serving as well as in suffering. Amen.

We really cannot compare one type of suffering to another. Some have physical pain; others suffer emotionally for Christ. Some sufferings may seem mild to a few people and actually are agonizing to others. And what seems an awful infliction of pain may not hurt the physically strong. Whenever Paul suffered outwardly, he rejoiced in his suffering because he knew Christ, served Christ, was sent by Christ, and was doing ministry for Christ.

Lord, there have been difficult days and losses. There has been pain and emotionally intensive suffering. Thank You for the privilege of suffering for You. Amen.

Read: 2 Corinthians 6:1-18

DAY 36

NO SECOND CHANCE

It is appointed unto men once to die

(Hebrews 9:27, KJV).

Each person is destined to die once

(Hebrews 9:27, NLT).

Death comes once, and you don't get a second chance to live again on this earth. In the same way, each moment of time comes once, and you cannot relive that moment again. That means there is no second chance after death. Think of some things you buy that can only be used once. Some of those products are manufactured to be thrown away after just one use. A gift certificate can only be used once to buy a gift. But the happiness you gave with the gift you purchased will live on. Now think of your time as a gift certificate. God gives you time/gift certificates. You can use it profitably or throw it away. Remember, time can be used only once.

Lord, teach me the value of time. I do not want to waste my life. I want to be influential for You. Help me discipline my time, guard my time, use my time, and when given the opportunity, help me invest my time for Your eternal privilege. Amen.

Think of time as an opportunity to take a trip or visit some place you have always wanted to see. You will only get there once. So make sure you see it all, experience it all, and enjoy it all—because you will never come back. Time is like that—you will never live that moment of time again. Oh you may get to return, but the second trip is not the same as the first trip. So get as much as you can out of each moment of time you have on earth.

Lord, help me to see all I should see, experience all I should experience, and become all You want me to become. Death is coming; I don't want to leave any wasted time behind. Amen.

Read: Hebrews 9:24-28; Luke 16:19-31

DAY 37

DEATH AND SORROW

But now he is dead; why should I fast? Can I bring him back again? I shall go to him, but he shall not return to me

(2 Samuel 12:23).

David faced the harsh reality of life and death. His little baby had died, even though David fasted and prayed for the child to live. The reality is death ends life on this earth, but life doesn't stop there—only physical life stops at death. David had wept parental tears when his baby was facing death. Now, look at the future. David realized, "he shall not return to me." It is always traumatic when you or anyone faces the death of a loved one. But look on the bright side—look on Heaven's side—you can see them again in Heaven. David said, "I shall go to him." For anyone who has lost a child in death, those babies who die before the age of accountability will go to Heaven.

Lord, death ends this life, but little babies will live with You in Heaven. Also, all who know Christ will live with You in Heaven. I look forward to Heaven, but first I have work and a life to live on earth. Help me to live for You and complete Your plan for my life. Amen.

Most everyone cries at a funeral. It is hard to think of being separated from those we know and love. Sometimes it is hard because we don't know if the one who died is with God in Heaven. Also, we think of our loss—the one who died will not be there for us. They leave an empty hole in our life and heart. Yes, death ends their life on earth, but their memory lives on. So does our love for them, and we will continue to miss and love them. So death does not end it for us.

Lord, I praise You for loved ones who died and went to Heaven. Even though I miss them, repair the hurt in my heart. But I am glad they live with You in Heaven. Amen.

Read: 2 Samuel 12:1-25

DAY 38

NOW IS A GOOD TIME

Seventy years are given to us! Some even live to eighty. But even the best years are filled with pain and trouble; soon they disappear, and we fly away

(Psalm 90:10, NLT).

Our life is short. The psalmist suggested some will live 70 years before they die. That is an average lifespan, but some die earlier by sickness, accident, or other reasons. Then the writer suggested, "Some even live to eighty." No one knows how old they will be at death, and no one knows when death is coming. Therefore, live this day to the Lord. Do all you are supposed to do, do it on time, and do it as best you can. You don't know if you will be alive tomorrow. Serve God with all your heart this day; it may be your last one. Also, do your best because you serve God. Give Him your best whether you will live a long time or it is the final day—*finish well!*

Lord, You invented time when You created the heavens and the earth, when You began everything. One day I will give an account to You for how I have spent my time. Help me redeem the time (Ephesians 5:16). Help me make the most of every opportunity. Amen.

Once you have used a minute or an hour or day, you will never get it back. You can never use lost time. Why? Because it is lost, gone, vanished.

So plan to get the most out of the next minute, hour, day. You cannot redeem lost time—it is gone—but you can redeem all your future time.

> *Lord, teach me the value of redeeming my time now and in the future. Then teach me how to do it—making the most of all my time. Lord, motivate me to start now, so I won't lose more time in the future. Help me start now—Lord, I love that word "now"! Amen.*

Read: Ephesians 5:15-20; Psalm 90:1-12

DAY 39

WISELY USE YOUR TIME

Teach us to realize the brevity of life, so that we may grow in wisdom
(Psalm 90:12, NLT).

The psalmist prayed for God to teach us "the brevity of life." Why would he pray that? He wouldn't be afraid of dying, so he doesn't pray to not die, or not die in pain, or to prolong life. The psalmist prayed for God to teach him about the brevity of life for many positive reasons. First, he may want to do as much as possible before he meets death. But it may be more specific; he may have certain things he must do before he dies, and he is asking for enough time to do them. Perhaps it is not about finishing any project or goal. Maybe the psalmist is asking God to help him to *finish well*. That is the theme of this book.

> *Lord, I know life is brief and death will come when I "fly away" into Your presence. Help me do all the things You want me to accomplish before the end comes. I want to be ready when death comes. Amen.*

Perhaps the psalmist is asking God to help him walk wisely and quickly. Why? Because death is in our datebook, and our time to die gets closer each day. We must work each day as if it is our last day. In other words, make each day count! One last thing, the psalmist wants us to "grow in wisdom." Isn't using your time well a wise thing?

Lord, teach me to use all my time well. May I use my next hour well! Also, my next day, next year, next decade! I want to use my time wisely so I can be wise. Amen.

Read: Proverbs 7:1-27

DAY 40

HOW OLD IS GOD?

Lord, through all the generations you have been our home! Before the mountains were born, before you gave birth to the earth and the world, from beginning to end, you are God

(Psalm 90:1-2, NLT).

When you think about your time, or the amount of time you have left before you die, ask, "How old is God?" The passage today describes God living before the mountains were created or the earth was created. Yes, God existed thousands of years ago when He created the heavens and the earth (Genesis 1:1). But beyond that, God has always lived/existed. He is eternal: *"from everlasting to everlasting thou art God"* (Psalm 90:2, KJV). Then God created the earth, animals, and the first humans, and their life started. But God's life never started—He has always existed. He is eternal!

God, I bow to thank You for giving me life through my parents. Thank You for my past, but most of all thank You for protecting/ leading me to this hour. Then too, I cannot forget the future. Lead me, protect me, and bring me home to live with You when I die. Amen.

How old is God? *"A thousand years in thy sight are but as yesterday"* (Psalm 90:4, KJV). Then the psalmist prayed, *"Satisfy us each morning with Your unfailing love, so we may sing for joy to the end of our days"*

(Psalm 90:14, ELT). No matter how old God is, His love for us is just as old. It endures, and God will keep on loving us until we die. Then in Heaven we will enjoy His love, as we in turn give Him our love.

Lord God, You are the eternal Creator, but more than that You have eternal love for all people—for me. For You, God, so loved me that You sent Jesus Christ Your Son to die for my sins. Amen.

Read: Genesis 1:1-27; John 3:14-21

DAY 41

OPPORTUNITIES

So be careful how you live. Don't live like fools, but like those who are wise

(Ephesians 5:15, NLT).

If you don't use your time wisely, you will lose it. What do you lose? You lose the opportunity to do something profitable for you, your family, your friends, for God. We all have only a few days, or a few years, or a few decades to live. So use your time wisely. If you don't do as the Bible says and number your days, you will not accomplish much. Those who goof off in school will not get an education. The new employee who does a "halfway job" will not be promoted or get ahead in life. The husband or wife who doesn't invest in their marriage doesn't find the happiness in life they seek. The Bible directs you to make the most of every opportunity.

Lord, give me Your eyes to see opportunities, then give me Your heart to pray and seek that opportunity. Next, I need Your determination to use that opportunity. Finally, I ask for Your blessing in all I do. Help me make every opportunity count for this life and Your glory. Amen.

When the Bible challenges us "to number our days," it means to plan to use them profitability. Think of a child counting the coins in their piggy bank to get the thing they want to buy. In the same way, your "coin" to purchase things is your time to serve God. Is your body a "piggy bank" that contains precious coins/time that can be used profitably? Use every opportunity or you will lost it.

> *Lord, give me Your eyes to see the value of my time. Remind me how valuable my time is. Help me plan to use my time correctly and help me spend/use my time for Your glory. And Lord, help me not waste my time. Amen.*

Read: Ephesians 5:1-21

DAY 42

MAKE TIME COUNT

Teach us to number our days

(Psalm 90:12).

If life is like a race, each runner will consider the distance to the finish line. If life is like a job, workers will count the time to quitting time. If life is money, we will count how much we have in the bank, how much we owe, how much we have left over after paying our bills, and how much we will spend on ourselves for pleasure. Since life is time, we ought to count our time we have left on earth. That is hard to do because we don't know when we will die. But we know death is inevitable, so count your time today, tomorrow, and every day until you go to meet God. Most workers look at the clock and ask, "How long till quitting time?" So how much time do you have left before "quitting time"?

> *Lord, help me make my time count for You. I want to do as much as I can until "quitting time." I want to be effective in what I do, and I want to do my best. Help me, guide me, strengthen me, use me. Amen.*

When you ask, "How much time do I have left?" you are examining the meaning of your life. Time is what you are, and your existence is measured by time. To make your life count, make your time count. To make your life meaningful, make your time meaningful. To make your life valuable, make your time influential for now, for the next moment, forever.

Lord, use me, use my time. Use my life to count for You, and I will use my time for Your glory. Help me number my days because time counts. Amen.

Read: Proverbs 8:1-36

DAY 43

WHEN YOU HAVE FINISHED WELL

When your life is challenged and you moved into action to satisfy the demands of your challenge, then you have *finished well*.

When you have completed all that is required of you and you are satisfied that you have done your best and you have completed the job, then you have *finished well*.

When you have done all that those over you have asked and/or expected and you know they are satisfied with your work, then you have *finished well*.

When you know what the public expects of you and you have completed the task they expected you to finish and you fulfilled their expectations, then you have *finished well*.

When the vison is finished that motivated you to launch out on the project God put upon your heart and you have done what the vision expected, then you have *finished well*.

When the burden that motivated you to work, sacrifice, and endure suffering is lifted because you have completed what you have begun, then you have *finished well*.

SERMON/TEACHING OUTLINES

Lesson 1: Grandpa Jacob Blessed His Grandchildren

A. Introduction: Jacob Grew Into a Trickster

1. Tricked his older brother Esau out of the birthright (family name and privilege). *"Sell me your birthright"* (Genesis 25:31), pride and stew meat.

2. Tricked Esau out of inheritance (wealth). Told Rebekah his mother, *"Esau is hairy, I am smooth-skinned"* (Genesis 27:11, ELT). Price, hairy, long sleeve jacket.

3. Tricked uncle Laban. Natural born sheep versus streaked, speckled, spotted.

4. While living/working for Laban—twelve sons and one daughter sneaked away. Mizpah Benediction: *"May the Lord watch between you and me when we are absent one from another"* (Genesis 31:49).

5. Elderly Jacob told his grandchildren of God's blessings.

> *God almighty appeared to me at Luz...blessed me, "Behold, I the Lord will prosper you in all you do. I will give you many children and you will become a great nation. I the Lord promise this land to you—a Promised Land—that you should inherit this land for an everlasting possession"* (Genesis 48:3-4, ELT).

6. Law of second born given first generation privilege. Jacob, second born, before Esau, first born.

B. Four Things Grandpa Jacob Gave His Grandchildren

1. <u>Adopted</u> them. Both boys had an Egyptian mother. "*Your two sons, Ephraim and Manasseh...shall be mine*" (Genesis 48:5).

2. Gave them his <u>name</u>. "*Let my name be upon them...Abraham and Isaac*" (Genesis 48:16, ELT).

3. Gave them God's <u>future</u>. "*Let them grow into a multitude*" (Genesis 48:16).

4. Gave them an example of <u>worship</u>. First, "*He bowed down with his face to the earth*" (Genesis 48:12). Second, "*He leaned on his staff continually to bless*" (Hebrews 11:21, ELT).

C. Old Testament Blessings on Children

1. A meaningful <u>touch</u>. Hand on their heads.

2. Bless with <u>spoken word</u>. Let them hear God's promise.

3. Attach <u>high value</u> to the one being blessed. Tell them what you/God expects of them.

4. <u>Picture</u>—a special future for them. "'*I know the plans I have for you,*' says the Lord. '*They are plans for good and not for disaster, to give you a future and a hope*'" (Jeremiah 29:11, NLT).

5. Active <u>commitment</u> to fulfill the blessing in their future.

D. To Take Away

1. You must be concerned about your children's <u>future</u>, grandchildren, great-grandchildren, etc.

2. You must be a spiritual <u>example</u> of godliness.

3. You must give them your <u>testimony</u>.

4. You must <u>determine</u> a time, place, and event to do it.

Lesson 2: Grandma Naomi Influenced Generations

A. How Naomi Compromised

1. She compromised her <u>spiritual priorities</u>.
   a. Did not continue in difficulties. "A famine in the land" (Ruth 1:1).
   b. Enticed by the well-watered plains of Moab (1:1).
   c. Left the Promised Land. "Ephrathites of Bethlehem, Judah" (1:2).
2. She compromised her commitment <u>to the Lord</u>. When Ruth, her daughter-in-law, wanted to go with Naomi, she directed Ruth to go back to her foreign gods. *"Look, your sister-in-law has gone back to her people and to her gods; return after your sister-in-law"* (1:15).
3. Naomi compromised her <u>family influence</u>. Naomi's son, Chilion, married outside the faith (1:4).
4. Naomi ended up <u>bitter about</u> God's provision. *"I went out full, and the Lord has brought me home again empty"* (1:21). *"Call me Mara, for the Almighty has dealt very bitterly with me"* (1:20).

B. What Naomi Did Right

1. <u>Naomi recognized God's punishment</u>. *"The Lord hath caused me to suffer and the Almighty has sent such tragedy"* (1:21, NLT).
2. <u>Naomi's counsel toward family heritage</u>. When Ruth "happened" on Boaz's field, Naomi said, *"'Blessed be he of the Lord, who has not forsaken His kindness to the living and the dead!' And Naomi said to her, 'This man is a relation of ours, one of our close relatives'"* (2:20).

3. Naomi counseled toward <u>redemption</u>. "*Then Naomi her mother-in-law said to her, 'My daughter, shall I not seek security for you, that it may be well with you?'*" (3:1).

4. Naomi counseled <u>patience and trust</u>. "*Then she* [Naomi] *said, 'Sit still, my daughter...for the man will not rest until he has concluded the matter this day'*" (3:18).

C. THE BLESSING OF NAOMI

Then the women said to Naomi, "Blessed be the Lord, who has not left you this day without a close relative; and may his name be famous in Israel! And may he be to you a restorer of life and a nourisher of your old age; for your daughter-in-law, who loves you, who is better to you than seven sons, has borne him"

(Ruth 4:14–15).

1. Naomi is given <u>more importance</u> in the Bible than Ruth.
   a. The women blessed Naomi (4:14).
   b. The child is recognized as "kin" to Naomi (4:14).
   c. Naomi had oversight for the child's care (4:16).
2. The child is <u>identified</u> with this grandmother (not father or grandfather). Note: legal line not through Naomi and Elimelech (4:21).
3. The child Obed would be <u>famous in Israel</u>.
   a. The word *famous* means "name is proclaimed widely."
   b. Obed was the <u>grandfather</u> of King David.
   c. Obed comes from two words, 1) Obadiah i.e., a <u>worshiper of God</u>; 2) *ebed*, i.e., <u>servant</u>. Obed was a true servant and worshiper of the Lord.
4. The child gave Grandmother Naomi a <u>purpose in life</u>.
   a. Naomi had been a <u>compromiser</u>, but she became a woman of <u>conviction</u>.
   b. Naomi didn't have <u>any hope</u>. She told Ruth, "*Turn back, my daughters, go—for I am too old to have a husband. If I should say I have*

hope, if I should have a husband tonight and should also bear sons" (1:12). But God gave her a <u>new life</u>. "*He* [Obed] *shall be unto thee a restorer of thy life*" (4:15, KJV).

    c. Naomi had no <u>spiritual energy</u>. "*Call me Mara: for the Almighty hath dealt very bitterly with me*" (1:20, KJV). But Obed <u>nourished</u> her old age. "*And may he* [Obed] *be to you a restorer of life and a nourisher of your old age*" (4:15).

5. Naomi gained <u>the love</u> of her daughter-in-law. "*Then the women said to Naomi, 'Blessed be the Lord...for your daughter-in-law, who loves you, who is better to you than seven sons*" (4:14-15).

6. Naomi had the responsibility of <u>influencing</u> the child.

    a. Naomi was given a <u>second chance</u> to rear a son.

    b. A rich man like Boaz would need <u>a nanny</u> for children—he got Naomi. "*Then Naomi took the child and laid him on her bosom, and became a nurse to him*" (4:16).

D. LESSONS TO TAKE AWAY

1. God can <u>forgive</u> the sins and mistakes of your youth and use you in your old age.

2. You can list Naomi's mistakes, but we remember how God used her <u>in spite of them</u>.

3. What is the main lesson to learn from Naomi?

LESSON 3:
ELIJAH FINISHED WELL

A. ELIJAH ON HIS WAY TO THE FINISH LINE: 2 KINGS 2:1-10

1. About to <u>finish</u>. *"The Lord was about to take up Elijah into heaven"* (2 Kings 2:1).
   a. Everyone seemed to <u>know</u> (2:3,5,7).
   b. Many will <u>see</u> (2:15).
   c. Some did not think Elijah went to Heaven, but to a <u>mountain</u> (2:16-18).

2. Note the progression from Gilead to Bethel to Jericho to Jordan to <u>Heaven</u>:
   a. Moving away from a nation of idols that <u>provoked God</u>
   b. Cross Jordan, a symbol of physical death

3. A <u>secret</u> that everyone knew. *"Did you know the Lord is going to take your master away from you today? Yes, be quiet"* (2:3, ELT).

4. Jordan, a well-known figure of death.
   a. Elijah walked through <u>death without harm</u>.
   b. Chariot to Heaven pictures your future <u>rapture</u>. You can go to Heaven the way of Elijah.

5. Why did Elijah say to young Elisha, "Stay here"? To <u>test</u>.

6. Why did Elisha ask. *"Let a double portion of your spirit be upon me"* (2:9)?
   a. His inner <u>character</u>
   b. His <u>influence</u>
   c. His <u>miracles</u>

7. What is a double portion?
   a. Center stage of God's miracle
   b. <u>Leadership</u> of the prophets
   c. <u>Twice</u> the miracles

8. *"You have asked a hard thing"* (2:10). Why hard?
   a. Not for Elijah to <u>give</u>
   b. Hard for Elijah to <u>teach or give</u>
   c. Hard to <u>learn</u>

9. Angels take us to Heaven at death (Luke 16:22). Seraphim means <u>fiery</u>. *"God makes His angels flaming fire"* (Psalm 104:4, ELT).

10. Just as Elijah was alone in serving in life, he was <u>alone in the chariot</u> heading to Heaven.

11. Today's question is not, "Where is the Lord, the God of Elijah?" We know that answer. But, "Where are the <u>Elijahs</u> of the Lord God?"

B. TEN APPLICATIONS FOR FINISHING WELL

1. Life is more than faithfully running your race; it is important how you <u>finish</u>. God gave Elijah a great departure that expanded God's power.

2. As you spend a life walking with God, serving God, and trusting His power, your *finish* should experience God's <u>favor</u> and God's <u>reputation</u>.

3. Elijah told Elisha three times, "stay here" to <u>test</u> him. Did Elisha mean it when they first met (1 Kings 19:19-21)?

4. Sometimes you must minister <u>without help</u> just as Elijah. *"Fifty men of the sons of the prophets went and stood facing them at a distance"* (2:7).

5. Preparing to finish. *"Elijah folded his cloak, struck the water, the river divided, the two of them crossed over on dry land"* (2:8, ELT).

6. If you could ask for a double portion, whom would you ask? _____ How must you live, and what must you do to finish well? _____
    _____.

7. *"You have asked a hard thing"* (2:10). Why hard?
    a. Overcome <u>self-pride</u>
    b. Overcome <u>lust of flesh</u>
    c. Hard to get God's vision, <u>lust of eyes</u>
    d. "If you..." (2:10). The greatest challenge to you "if."

8. Elijah, who had a continuing battle with kings, went out as a <u>conqueror</u>. God does not send His chariot to a land filled with idols, but to the other side of Jordan.

9. It is good God doesn't answer all your <u>selfish prayers</u>. Elijah prayed, *"Take my life"* (1 Kings 19:4).

10. In Elijah's departure we have a picture of Christ coming for us, and we have His assurance He <u>can do it</u>.

Lesson 4: John, 90 Years Old, Finished Well

A. John Began Well

1. The apostle John was one of the <u>first called</u>. *"Two disciples followed Jesus. Andrew first found his brother and brought him to Jesus. John also found his brother. 'We have found the Messiah, the Christ'"* (John 1:38-41, ELT).

2. The youngest of the 12 disciples—<u>17 years old</u>
   a. Enthusiastic
   b. Exploring
   c. Self-centered—nicknamed "son of thunder" (Mark 3:17)
   d. Forbad people casting out demons (Luke 9:49-50)

3. Transformed into the <u>apostle of love</u>
   a. Loved by <u>Jesus</u> (John 13:23)
   b. Called self, *"the disciple whom Jesus loved"* (John 21:7)
   c. Known as apostle of love (1 John 4:7)

4. Transformed by <u>identifying</u> with Jesus; leaned on Jesus' breast (John 13:23-25)

5. Grew spiritual by <u>responsibly</u>
   a. *"Follow Me"* (John 21:19).
   b. Follow <u>Jesus</u>. *"He who says he abides in Him ought himself also to walk just as He walked"* (1 John 2:6).

6. <u>Expectation principles</u>: Jesus told John from the cross, "Take care of My mother." Jesus challenged young John to grow when He gave him the responsibly of caring for Mary, His mother.

7. Following continually—<u>finishing well</u>
   a. Began age 17

b. Followed Jesus three and a half years on earth

c. <u>Prayed</u> in the garden (Mark 14:3)

d. One betrayed, ten ran away, John followed <u>all night</u> (John 18:16)

e. At the foot of cross given the responsibility of Mary (John 19:26)

f. First at <u>tomb</u> (John 20:2-3)

g. First to <u>recognize</u> the resurrected Jesus (John 21:1-7)

h. Remained in Jerusalem during persecution (Acts 8:1)

i. Among the first to recognize Paul (Galatians 2:9)

8. Pastored/ministered to the church in Ephesus (traditionally, Mary mother of Jesus died there).

9. Arrested and imprisoned on Patmos, an island for political prisoners. *"I, John, your brother was on the island called Patmos for the Word of God and Jesus"* (Revelation 1:9, ELT).

B. JOHN SAW THE FUTURE

1. John <u>saw</u> Jesus. *"I heard behind me a loud voice...I turned to see One like the Son of God"* (Revelation 1:10-13, ELT). *"Do not be afraid; I am the First and the Last"* (Revelation 1:17).

2. John given a <u>commission</u>: *"I am He who lives, and was dead, and behold, I am alive forevermore. Amen. And I have the keys of Hades and of Death"* (Revelation 1:18).

3. John taken to Heaven in a <u>prophetic revelation</u>. *"I looked, and behold, a door standing open in heaven.... 'Come up here, and I will show you'"* (Revelation 4:1).

4. John saw the <u>second coming of Jesus</u> (Revelation 19:11, 14).

5. John saw Heaven. *"I saw a new heaven and new earth"* (Revelation 21:1).

6. God's eternal <u>presence</u>. *"The tabernacle of God is with men, and He will dwell with them.... God Himself will be with them and be their God"* (Revelation 21:3).

7. All evil <u>gone</u>. *"No more death, nor sorrow, nor crying. There shall be no more pain, for the former things have passed away"* (Revelation 21:4).

LESSON 5: PAUL FINISHED WHAT HE FIRST BEGAN

A. PAUL DID NOT START WELL

1. Paul was completely committed to <u>keeping</u> the Old Testament Law. He was circumcised at eight days old, a pure-blooded citizen of Israel, of the tribe of Benjamin, a Pharisee, demanded strictest obedience, and harshly persecuted the church (Philippians 3:5-6, NLT).

2. <u>Persecuted</u> the church. *"But Saul was going everywhere to destroy the church. He went from house to house, dragging out both men and women to throw them into prison"* (Acts 8:3, NLT).

3. <u>Murder</u>. *"Eager to kill the Lord's followers"* (Acts 9:1, NLT).

B. INTRODUCTION: PAUL'S DREAM FINISH INVOLVED AT LEAST THREE AREAS

1. To finish the <u>Great Commission</u>.

2. To be <u>conformed</u> to likeness of Jesus Christ.

3. Serve faithfully to <u>death/rapture</u>.

C. COMPLETE THE GREAT COMMISSION (FOUR PARTS)

1. No <u>person</u> left out. *"God wants everyone to repent"* (2 Peter 3:4, ELT).

2. No <u>people groups</u> left out. *"Go make disciples of every [ethna] people group"* (Matthew 28:19, ELT).

3. No <u>place</u> left out. "*To preach the Good News where the name of Christ has never been heard*" (Romans 15:20, NLT).

4. No <u>language</u> left out. "*This message would be proclaimed to all people groups*" (Luke 24:47, ELT).

5. Paul's <u>personal</u> commitment. "*I have been following the plan...those who have never been told about him will see, and those who have never heard of him will understand*" (Romans 15:21, NLT).

D. To Be Conformed to the Image of Jesus Christ

1. <u>Died</u> with Christ: "*I have been crucified with Christ; it is no longer I who live, but Christ lives in me; and the life which I now live in the flesh I live by faith in the Son of God, who loved me and gave Himself for me*" (Galatians 2:20).

2. To <u>know</u> Christ: "*that I may know Him and the power of His resurrection, and the fellowship of His sufferings, being conformed to His death*" (Philippians 3:10).

3. <u>Made</u> like Christ: "*I press on to receive that perfection for which Christ Jesus first possessed me...I press to reach the end of the race and receive the heavenly prize*" (Philippians 3:14, ELT).

E. To Be Faithful to Death

I press toward the goal for the prize of the upward call of God in Christ Jesus (Philippians 3:14).

1. Tradition—Paul died on flaming torch in Nero's garden in the 60s A.D.

2. Paul's <u>commitment</u>: "*My life has already been poured out as an offering to God...I have fought the good fight, I have finished the race, and I have remained faithful. And now the prize awaits me—the crown of righteousness*" (2 Timothy 4:6-8, NLT).

Lesson 6: Your Time to Finish Well

A. Measuring Time to Finish Well

1. What is involved in finishing well?
    a. On <u>time</u>
    b. Excellence
    c. Cover all <u>details</u>
    d. Includes all <u>people involved</u>
2. You are <u>registered</u> for the race of life, and you are <u>running</u>.
3. You have been given gifts:
    a. Like money, spend it well.
    b. Like stocks and bonds, <u>invest it well</u>.
    c. Like your health, <u>nourish it</u> well.
    d. Time, use it profitably and prayerfully.

What Is Time?

- <u>Sequence</u> of events in irreversible succession
- Measurements of <u>events</u> by a clock
- Mathematical <u>tool</u> to organize and perform events
- Continual <u>flow</u> of people and events, from past history to the future

4. God included time's technical definition: "*In the beginning God created the heavens and the earth*" (Genesis 1:1).
    a. <u>Previously</u> there was no time.
    b. He created time in an instant and it continues.

B. What Does Time Mean to Us?

1. Time is <u>life</u>. *"What is your life? It is even a vapor that appears for a little time and then vanishes"* (James 4:14). Life is time.

2. When time is gone/spent, it <u>never comes back</u>. *"People are like grass that springs up in the morning, and in evening it dies"* (Psalm 90:5-6, ELT).

3. Human time moves to a <u>conclusion</u>: "Seventy years" (Psalm 90:10).

4. Humans are born in time and are captives of time, but <u>not God</u>. *"A thousand years are but as yesterday to you! They are like a single hour!"* (Psalm 90:4, TLB).

C. Don't Count Time—Make Time Count

1. *"Teach us to count our days, so we can wisely use time"* (Psalm 90:12, ELT). Children count the time to recess as <u>slow</u>. For elders, time <u>gallops</u>.

2. Time passes quickly; you never know when the end comes. Our time is carried away like a flood (Psalm 90:5).

3. David and Bathsheba's baby boy died (2 Samuel 12:23).

D. Count Your Time—No Second Change

1. Count means to:
   a. Identify
   b. Plan
   c. Know your <u>goals</u>
   d. Know your assets (strengths)
   e. Know your <u>weaknesses</u>
   f. Know <u>opposition</u>
   g. Evaluate options
   h. Execute

2. You never get back time <u>spent</u>, money spent, water drunk.

E. INVESTING YOUR TIME IS FINISHING WELL

1. Time is opportunity. What would you do if you only had:
   a. One <u>visit</u>
   b. One meeting
   c. One ceremony
   d. Last <u>speech</u>
2. Two uses:
   a. <u>Waiting</u> time—plan, meditate, pray, rejuvenate
   b. <u>Wasting</u> time—do nothing, think nothing
3. Spent time, like spent money, cannot be used again. *"Life is not measured by the things you own"* (Luke 12:15, ELT).

F. INVESTING YOUR TIME IS FINISHING WELL

1. Criminal on death row to be executed receives good news: "Your uncle left you an inheritance of a million dollars." <u>Too late to use it</u>.
2. Even pain and affliction teaches us lessons. *"Our light affliction are small and will only last on the earth, in Heaven everything will be different"* (2 Corinthians 4:17, ELT).
3. If you don't use time profitably:
   a. <u>Little</u> done
   b. Lost <u>opportunity</u>: "Use it or lose it."
   c. Pay now or <u>pay later</u>.
   d. You dishonor God who gave you time.
   e. You lose <u>control</u> of your future.
4. You hold the <u>deposit slip</u> of time given you. You have the assets of time. Good stewards <u>manage well</u>.

LISTENER OUTLINES

LESSON 1: GRANDPA JACOB BLESSED HIS GRANDCHILDREN

A. INTRODUCTION: JACOB GREW INTO A TRICKSTER

1. Tricked his older brother Esau out of the birthright (family name and _____). *"Sell me your birthright"* (Genesis 25:31), _____ and stew meat.

2. Tricked Esau out of inheritance (_____). Told Rebekah his mother, *"Esau is hairy, I am smooth-skinned"* (Genesis 27:11, ELT). Price, hairy, long sleeve _____.

3. Tricked uncle Laban. _____ born sheep versus streaked, speckled, spotted.

4. While living/working for Laban—twelve sons and one daughter _____. Mizpah Benediction: *"May the Lord watch between you and me when we are absent one from another"* (Genesis 31:49).

5. Elderly Jacob told his grandchildren of God's _____.

> *God almighty appeared to me at Luz...blessed me, "Behold, I the Lord will prosper you in all you do. I will give you many children and you will become a great nation. I the Lord promise this land to you—a Promised Land—that you should inherit this land for an everlasting possession"* (Genesis 48:3-4, ELT).

6. Law of _____ given first generation privilege. Jacob, second born, before Esau, first born.

B. FOUR THINGS GRANDPA JACOB GAVE HIS GRANDCHILDREN

1. _____ them. Both boys had an Egyptian mother. *"Your two sons, Ephraim and Manasseh...shall be mine"* (Genesis 48:5).

2. Gave them his _____. *"Let my name be upon them...Abraham and Isaac"* (Genesis 48:16, ELT).

3. Gave them God's _____. *"Let them grow into a multitude"* (Genesis 48:16).

4. Gave them an example of _____. First, *"He bowed down with his face to the earth"* (Genesis 48:12). Second, *"He leaned on his staff continually to bless"* (Hebrews 11:21, ELT).

C. OLD TESTAMENT BLESSINGS ON CHILDREN

1. A meaningful _____. Hand on their heads.

2. Bless with _____. Let them hear God's promise.

3. Attach _____ to the one being blessed. Tell them what you/God expects of them.

4. _____—a special future for them. *"'I know the plans I have for you,' says the Lord. 'They are plans for good and not for disaster, to give you a future and a hope'"* (Jeremiah 29:11, NLT).

5. Active _____ to fulfill the blessing in their future.

D. TO TAKE AWAY

1. You must be concerned about your children's _____, grandchildren, great-grandchildren, etc.

2. You must be a spiritual _____ of godliness.

3. You must give them your _____.

4. You must _____ a time, place, and event to do it.

Lesson 2: Grandma Naomi Influenced Generations

A. How Naomi Compromised

1. She compromised her _____.
   a. Did not continue in difficulties. "A famine in the land" (Ruth 1:1).
   b. Enticed by the well-watered plains of Moab (1:1).
   c. Left the Promised Land. "Ephrathites of Bethlehem, Judah" (1:2).
2. She compromised her commitment _____. When Ruth, her daughter-in-law, wanted to go with Naomi, she directed Ruth to go back to her foreign gods. "*Look, your sister-in-law has gone back to her people and to her gods; return after your sister-in-law*" (1:15).
3. Naomi compromised her _____. Naomi's son, Chilion, married outside the faith (1:4).
4. Naomi ended up _____ God's provision. "*I went out full, and the Lord has brought me home again empty*" (1:21). "*Call me Mara, for the Almighty has dealt very bitterly with me*" (1:20).

B. What Naomi Did Right

1. _____. "*The Lord hath caused me to suffer and the Almighty has sent such tragedy*" (1:21, NLT).
2. _____. When Ruth "happened" on Boaz's field, Naomi said, "'*Blessed be he of the Lord, who has not forsaken His kindness to the living and the dead!' And Naomi said to her, 'This man is a relation of ours, one of our close relatives*'" (2:20).

3. Naomi counseled toward _____. *"Then Naomi her mother-in-law said to her, 'My daughter, shall I not seek security for you, that it may be well with you?'"* (3:1).

4. Naomi counseled _____. *"Then she [Naomi] said, 'Sit still, my daughter...for the man will not rest until he has concluded the matter this day'"* (3:18).

C. THE BLESSING OF NAOMI

Then the women said to Naomi, "Blessed be the Lord, who has not left you this day without a close relative; and may his name be famous in Israel! And may he be to you a restorer of life and a nourisher of your old age; for your daughter-in-law, who loves you, who is better to you than seven sons, has borne him"

(Ruth 4:14–15).

1. Naomi is given _____ in the Bible than Ruth.
   a. The women blessed Naomi (4:14).
   b. The child is recognized as "kin" to Naomi (4:14).
   c. Naomi had oversight for the child's care (4:16).

2. The child is _____ with this grandmother (not father or grandfather). Note: legal line not through Naomi and Elimelech (4:21).

3. The child Obed would be _____.
   a. The word *famous* means "name is proclaimed widely."
   b. Obed was the _____ of King David.
   c. Obed comes from two words, 1) Obadiah i.e., a _____; 2) *ebed*, i.e., _____. Obed was a true servant and worshiper of the Lord.

4. The child gave Grandmother Naomi a _____.
   a. Naomi had been a _____, but she became a woman of _____.
   b. Naomi didn't have _____. She told Ruth, *"Turn back, my daughters, go—for I am too old to have a husband. If I should say I*

have hope, if I should have a husband tonight and should also bear sons" (1:12). But God gave her a _____. *"He [Obed] shall be unto thee a restorer of thy life"* (4:15, KJV).

   c. Naomi had no _____. *"Call me Mara: for the Almighty hath dealt very bitterly with me"* (1:20, KJV). But Obed _____ her old age. *"And may he [Obed] be to you a restorer of life and a nourisher of your old age"* (4:15).

5. Naomi gained _____ of her daughter-in-law. *"Then the women said to Naomi, 'Blessed be the Lord...for your daughter-in-law, who loves you, who is better to you than seven sons"* (4:14-15).

6. Naomi had the responsibility of _____ the child.

   a. Naomi was given a _____ to rear a son.

   b. A rich man like Boaz would need _____ for children—he got Naomi. *"Then Naomi took the child and laid him on her bosom, and became a nurse to him"* (4:16).

D. LESSONS TO TAKE AWAY

1. God can _____ the sins and mistakes of your youth and use you in your old age.

2. You can list Naomi's mistakes, but we remember how God used her _____.

3. What is the main lesson to learn from Naomi?

LESSON 3: ELIJAH FINISHED WELL

A. ELIJAH ON HIS WAY TO THE FINISH LINE: 2 KINGS 2:1-10

1. About to _____. *"The Lord was about to take up Elijah into heaven"* (2 Kings 2:1).
   a. Everyone seemed to _____ (2:3,5,7).
   b. Many will _____ (2:15).
   c. Some did not think Elijah went to Heaven, but to a _____ (2:16-18).

2. Note the progression from Gilead to Bethel to Jericho to Jordan to _____:
   a. Moving away from a nation of idols that _____
   b. Cross Jordan, a symbol of physical death

3. A _____ that everyone knew. *"Did you know the Lord is going to take your master away from you today? Yes, be quiet"* (2:3, ELT).

4. Jordan, a well-known figure of death.
   a. Elijah walked through _____.
   b. Chariot to Heaven pictures your future _____. You can go to Heaven the way of Elijah.

5. Why did Elijah say to young Elisha, "Stay here"? To _____.

6. Why did Elisha ask. *"Let a double portion of your spirit be upon me"* (2:9)?
   a. His inner _____
   b. His _____
   c. His _____

7. What is a double portion?
   a. Center stage of God's miracle
   b. _____ of the prophets
   c. _____ the miracles
8. *"You have asked a hard thing"* (2:10). Why hard?
   a. Not for Elijah to _____
   b. Hard for Elijah to _____
   c. Hard to _____
9. Angels take us to Heaven at death (Luke 16:22). Seraphim means _____. *"God makes His angels flaming fire"* (Psalm 104:4, ELT).
10. Just as Elijah was alone in serving in life, he was _____ heading to Heaven.
11. Today's question is not, "Where is the Lord, the God of Elijah?" We know that answer. But, "Where are the _____ of the Lord God?"

B. TEN APPLICATIONS FOR FINISHING WELL

1. Life is more than faithfully running your race; it is important how you _____. God gave Elijah a great departure that expanded God's power.
2. As you spend a life walking with God, serving God, and trusting His power, your *finish* should experience God's _____ and God's _____.
3. Elijah told Elisha three times, "stay here" to _____him. Did Elisha mean it when they first met (1 Kings 19:19-21)?
4. Sometimes you must minister _____ just as Elijah. *"Fifty men of the sons of the prophets went and stood facing them at a distance"* (2:7).
5. Preparing to finish. *"Elijah folded his cloak, struck the water, the river divided, the two of them crossed over on dry land"* (2:8, ELT).

6. If you could ask for a double portion, whom would you ask? _____
_____ How must you live, and what
must you do to finish well? _____
_____.

7. *"You have asked a hard thing"* (2:10). Why hard?
   a. Overcome _____
   b. Overcome _____
   c. Hard to get God's vision, _____
   d. "If you..." (2:10). The greatest challenge to you "if."

8. Elijah, who had a continuing battle with kings, went out as a
_____. God does not send His chariot to a land filled with
idols, but to the other side of Jordan.

9. It is good God doesn't answer all your _____. Elijah prayed,
"Take my life" (1 Kings 19:4).

10. In Elijah's departure we have a picture of Christ coming for us, and
we have His assurance He _____.

LESSON 4: JOHN, 90 YEARS OLD, FINISHED WELL

A. JOHN BEGAN WELL

1. The apostle John was one of the _____. *"Two disciples followed Jesus. Andrew first found his brother and brought him to Jesus. John also found his brother. 'We have found the Messiah, the Christ'"* (John 1:38-41, ELT).

2. The youngest of the 12 disciples—_____
   a. Enthusiastic
   b. Exploring
   c. Self-centered—nicknamed "son of thunder" (Mark 3:17)
   d. Forbad people casting out demons (Luke 9:49-50)

3. Transformed into the _____
   a. Loved by _____ (John 13:23)
   b. Called self, *"the disciple whom Jesus loved"* (John 21:7)
   c. Known as apostle of love (1 John 4:7)

4. Transformed by _____ with Jesus; leaned on Jesus' breast (John 13:23-25)

5. Grew spiritual by _____
   a. *"Follow Me"* (John 21:19).
   b. Follow _____. *"He who says he abides in Him ought himself also to walk just as He walked"* (1 John 2:6).

6. _____: Jesus told John from the cross, "Take care of My mother." Jesus challenged young John to grow when He gave him the responsibly of caring for Mary, His mother.

7. Following continually _____
   a. Began age 17

    b. Followed Jesus three and a half years on earth

    c. _____in the garden (Mark 14:3)

    d. One betrayed, ten ran away, John followed _____ (John 18:16)

    e. At the foot of cross given the responsibility of Mary (John 19:26)

    f. First at _____ (John 20:2-3)

    g. First to _____the resurrected Jesus (John 21:1-7)

    h. Remained in Jerusalem during persecution (Acts 8:1)

    i. Among the first to recognize Paul (Galatians 2:9)

8. Pastored/ministered to the church in Ephesus (traditionally, Mary mother of Jesus died there).

9. Arrested and imprisoned on Patmos, an island for political prisoners. *"I, John, your brother was on the island called Patmos for the Word of God and Jesus"* (Revelation 1:9, ELT).

B. JOHN SAW THE FUTURE

1. John _____Jesus. *"I heard behind me a loud voice...I turned to see One like the Son of God"* (Revelation 1:10-13, ELT). *"Do not be afraid; I am the First and the Last"* (Revelation 1:17).

2. John given a _____: *"I am He who lives, and was dead, and behold, I am alive forevermore. Amen. And I have the keys of Hades and of Death"* (Revelation 1:18).

3. John taken to Heaven in a _____. *"I looked, and behold, a door standing open in heaven.... 'Come up here, and I will show you'"* (Revelation 4:1).

4. John saw the _____(Revelation 19:11, 14).

5. John saw Heaven. *"I saw a new heaven and new earth"* (Revelation 21:1).

6. God's eternal _____. *"The tabernacle of God is with men, and He will dwell with them.... God Himself will be with them and be their God"* (Revelation 21:3).

7. All evil _____. *"No more death, nor sorrow, nor crying. There shall be no more pain, for the former things have passed away"* (Revelation 21:4).

Lesson 5: Paul Finished What He First Began

A. Paul Did Not Start Well

1. Paul was completely committed to _____ the Old Testament Law. He was circumcised at eight days old, a pure-blooded citizen of Israel, of the tribe of Benjamin, a Pharisee, demanded strictest obedience, and harshly persecuted the church (Philippians 3:5-6, NLT).

2. _____ the church. "*But Saul was going everywhere to destroy the church. He went from house to house, dragging out both men and women to throw them into prison*" (Acts 8:3, NLT).

3. _____. "*Eager to kill the Lord's followers*" (Acts 9:1, NLT).

B. Introduction: Paul's Dream Finish Involved at Least Three Areas

1. To finish the _____.
2. To be _____ to likeness of Jesus Christ.
3. Serve faithfully to _____.

C. Complete the Great Commission (Four Parts)

1. No _____ left out. "*God wants everyone to repent*" (2 Peter 3:4, ELT).

2. No _____ left out. "*Go make disciples of every [ethna] people group*" (Matthew 28:19, ELT).

3. No _____ left out. "*To preach the Good News where the name of Christ has never been heard*" (Romans 15:20, NLT).

4. No _____ left out. "*This message would be proclaimed to all people groups*" (Luke 24:47, ELT).

5. Paul's _____ commitment. "*I have been following the plan...those who have never been told about him will see, and those who have never heard of him will understand*" (Romans 15:21, NLT).

D. To Be Conformed to the Image of Jesus Christ

1. _____ with Christ: "*I have been crucified with Christ; it is no longer I who live, but Christ lives in me; and the life which I now live in the flesh I live by faith in the Son of God, who loved me and gave Himself for me*" (Galatians 2:20).

2. To _____ Christ: "*that I may know Him and the power of His resurrection, and the fellowship of His sufferings, being conformed to His death*" (Philippians 3:10).

3. _____ like Christ: "*I press on to receive that perfection for which Christ Jesus first possessed me...I press to reach the end of the race and receive the heavenly prize*" (Philippians 3:14, ELT).

E. To Be Faithful to Death

I press toward the goal for the prize of the upward call of God in Christ Jesus (Philippians 3:14).

1. Tradition—Paul died on flaming torch in Nero's garden in the 60s A.D.

2. Paul's _____: "*My life has already been poured out as an offering to God...I have fought the good fight, I have finished the race, and I have remained faithful. And now the prize awaits me—the crown of righteousness*" (2 Timothy 4:6-8, NLT).

LESSON 6: YOUR TIME TO FINISH WELL

A. MEASURING TIME TO FINISH WELL

1. What is involved in finishing well?
   a. On _____
   b. Excellence
   c. Cover all _____
   d. Includes all _____
2. You are _____ for the race of life, and you are _____.
3. You have been given gifts:
   a. Like money, spend it well.
   b. Like stocks and bonds, _____.
   c. Like your health, _____ well.
   d. Time, use it profitably and prayerfully.

WHAT IS TIME?

- _____ of events in irreversible succession
- Measurements of _____ by a clock
- Mathematical _____ to organize and perform events
- Continual _____ of people and events, from past history to the future

4. God included time's technical definition: *"In the beginning God created the heavens and the earth"* (Genesis 1:1).
   a. _____ there was no time.
   b. He created time in an instant and it continues.

B. What Does Time Mean to Us?

1. Time is _____. *"What is your life? It is even a vapor that appears for a little time and then vanishes"* (James 4:14). Life is time.

2. When time is gone/spent, it _____. *"People are like grass that springs up in the morning, and in evening it dies"* (Psalm 90:5-6, ELT).

3. Human time moves to a _____: "Seventy years" (Psalm 90:10).

4. Humans are born in time and are captives of time, but _____. *"A thousand years are but as yesterday to you! They are like a single hour!"* (Psalm 90:4, TLB).

C. Don't Count Time—Make Time Count

1. *"Teach us to count our days, so we can wisely use time"* (Psalm 90:12, ELT). Children count the time to recess as _____. For elders, time _____.

2. Time passes quickly; you never know when the end comes. Our time is carried away like a flood (Psalm 90:5).

3. David and Bathsheba's baby boy died (2 Samuel 12:23).

D. Count Your Time—No Second Change

1. Count means to:
   a. Identify
   b. Plan
   c. Know your _____
   d. Know your assets (strengths)
   e. Know your _____
   f. Know _____
   g. Evaluate options
   h. Execute

2. You never get back time _____, money spent, water drunk.

E. INVESTING YOUR TIME IS FINISHING WELL

1. Time is opportunity. What would you do if you only had:
   a. One _____
   b. One meeting
   c. One ceremony
   d. Last _____

2. Two uses:
   a. _____ time—plan, meditate, pray, rejuvenate
   b. _____ time—do nothing, think nothing

3. Spent time, like spent money, cannot be used again. *"Life is not measured by the things you own"* (Luke 12:15, ELT).

F. INVESTING YOUR TIME IS FINISHING WELL

1. Criminal on death row to be executed receives good news: "Your uncle left you an inheritance of a million dollars." _____.

2. Even pain and affliction teaches us lessons. *"Our light affliction are small and will only last on the earth, in Heaven everything will be different"* (2 Corinthians 4:17, ELT).

3. If you don't use time profitably:
   a. _____ done
   b. Lost _____: "Use it or lose it."
   c. Pay now or _____.
   d. You dishonor God who gave you time.
   e. You lose _____ of your future.

4. You hold the _____ of time given you. You have the assets of time. Good stewards _____.

ABOUT ELMER TOWNS

Dr. Elmer Towns has published more than 250 books, several of which have been accepted as college textbooks. He is also a recipient of the Gold Medallion Award awarded by the Christian Booksellers Association. He is co-founder of Liberty University, holds visiting professorship rank at five seminaries, and received six honorary doctoral degrees. He earned a BS from Northwestern College, an MA from Southern Methodist University, a ThM from Dallas Theological Seminary, an MRE from Garrett Theological Seminary, and a DMin from Fuller Theological Seminary.